THEFUTUREOFWORK

Make use of this book to lead the pack, not follow, and establish your proper place in the new market for work.

ROLF RITTER

www.PeopleAsAService.co/the-future-of-work

Miami, Florida

USA

Cover by Jefferson Quintana

Special Copyright Notice

Rolf Ritter. Part of a compilation, use of text that is greater than 5 percent of the book in which it will be quoted, or other permission requests shall be directed in writing to: For information, contact People as a Service, rolf.ritter@PeopleasaService.co

ISBN 978-0-9899573-4-2

Paperback edition

PRODUCED IN THE UNITED STATES OF

AMERICA

DEDICATION

To Mely, Farah and Luisa…

Loves of my life

ACKNOWLEDGMENTS

Part of this book has been based on my former book "Road to the Computer Age" and you will find some ideas represented in both books. I would therefore like to acknowledge everybody that has been part of "Road to the Computer Age" and, for this book, I would specifically like to thank Kitt Walsh for all her work that she has put into this book. Without her, there would most probably be no book at all and if there were it would never be as well written and clear as it is today. Thank you as well for all your input, criticism and great work to make this book a reality. I would like to thank Adriana Moreno for her input and criticism, and to Mely, my wife, and Farah and Luisa, my daughters, who show me every day what's truly important in life.

FOREWORD

I believe we are in a most interesting moment of modern civilization. It might not be apparent to most of us, but we are in the middle of a revolution comparable to the Industrial Revolution more than a century ago. During that period, not only did the economic system and the distribution of wealth change, but society as a whole underwent revolutionary change.

During the Industrial Revolution, society changed from an agrarian society, built around the land and the village, to an urban society built around value creation in a highly specialized manner—first through physical products and then through services.

In the agrarian phase, homesteaders and labors alike were able to handle every step of value creation on the farm—from growing food, harvesting, butchering and preparing the food to maintaining the needed infrastructure to complete the necessary tasks, while providing for everyone's needs, even the children, elderly and ill who were unable to offer heavy manual labor.

In contrast, today many people cannot even cook much less grow, harvest and prepare the food, which is the most basic of needs. Many would be hard-pressed to even outline the steps of food production.

In the present day's highly specialized society, governments, schools and corporations have built an organizing principle that allows for ever greater economies of scale and ever greater global specialization through highly organized hierarchical structure and detailed processes everyone is supposed to follow.

But now the time has come to throw this all over board and leave hundreds of years building hierarchical organizations behind and move to the new area of individual value creation on a global scale, where the organizing principle moves away from structure to results and from top management to individuals who create value. With these simple self-organizing structures, the future of work will be able to create more value with less effort and less waste. Individual talent will also flourish while limiting organizational structures will be replaced. Over time, the impact on society, government and public services like education and social security will be impacted on a fundamental level.

My ideas about this impact are contained in this short, easy-to-read book that I hope you will enjoy and which will give you some new ideas, insights, or questions about the future, which is about to begin.

Please visit www.PeopleAsAService.co/the-future-of-work and join the discussion about the Future of Work. Your input and comments are most welcome.

—Rolf Ritter

TABLE OF CONTENTS

INTRODUCTION

"Inventions have long since reached their limit,
and I see no hope for further developments."

—Julius Sextus Frontinus (40–103),
Roman engineer

Growth, productivity, and technological revolutions have been widely studied by economists, historians, and social scientists. These experts have done a great job in analyzing what has
happened, or what has not happened, and how
different areas are closely interconnected. I have
relied on some of those experts' findings when
researching this book because I believe there is
truth in the adage, "Those who forget history are
doomed to repeat it."

In every past revolution, those who resisted
changes that resulted in increased efficiency or
yields, less expenditure of talent and treasure for
greater profits or rewards, or systems that eventually benefitted more people, have been left behind
with the old order. On the other hand, those who
adapted themselves and their techniques with an
eye towards the often-rapid changes of the future,
found themselves on the right side of history, able

to not only survive the changes, but benefit from them. Individuals, companies and society as a whole gained from such adaptation.

In my career as a consultant, manager and CEO, I have spent a lot of time thinking about the future; how to improve the way companies work and how to put the talent within those companies to their best use. My thinking has evolved and that evolution forms the basis of my study detailed here.

In the beginning of my career, I believed that technology, like ERP systems and others to streamline processes, measure output and improve employee performance, were the right way to go. But the more I grew into management responsibilities and was faced with meeting challenges, I began to realize those tools often stand in the way of change and improvements as much or more than the people who depend on them. I realized that we have maneuvered our companies into a corner. We burdened them with unsatisfied employees, inflexible IT and management systems, overseen by the very managers who put their companies into such a corner in the first place—as they were most familiar with managing the broken system, instead of searching for a better way. This book will show you why we are in that position today and how to break out of it so we create a better world for employees and companies alike.

Technologies like the internet, Google, Wikipedia, TV-on-demand, the smartphone, and social media, have so influenced our lives we cannot imagine how we could live before they were introduced. However, looking at growth and productivity in long-term studies, unlike other technological revolutions, information technology has not left an overwhelming mark on economic growth—yet. I believe it will and by doing so, transform the very way we work and bring all of us many benefits.

We are living in the most extraordinary times of technology-driven revolution, which opens up both enormous opportunities and potential, as well as risks and changes, in every aspect of our lives. This book will show you what we have to do to avoid those pitfalls and realize those benefits—how we can create the future of work itself.

CHAPTER ONE

LOOKBACKWARDSTOMOVE FORWARDS

"Study the past, if you would divine the future."

—Confucius, Chinese teacher, politician,
philosopher

Revolution is bred into our very bones. As humans, overthrowing the status quo has been what allowed us to survive and evolve as a species.

From the moment our ancestor, Og, stepped from the cave, with a hand-fashioned spear, and decide to try to make use of that storm-brought fire from the sky and charbroil his meat instead of eating it raw, he started a revolution.

When his mate tried planting a seed instead of just gathering those already sprouted, easing her own labor and allowing her family to stay put through a growing season, she, too, changed the fabric of human lives forever.

When Whitney invented a cotton gin that did the work of hundreds of slaves and increased the production of cotton by a factor of 50, he, too, was starting a revolution.

The creation of a steam engine, improvements in iron production; new chemical processes to make glass, paper and cement; switching from devastating the forests for fuel to digging coal from the earth; all these launched a period where mankind went from doing everything by hand to mechanizing back-breaking tasks. The Industrial Revolution was born and the way we lived changed forever.

Revolutionaries like Carnegie and Edison and Ford blasted their way through "the way things always have been" to a future, seen at first only by them, to "the way things can be."

By changing the way we labor, these visionaries—and the legions more of chemists, industrialists, inventors and dreamers who looked beyond the current day—have changed the shape of history. By grasping or creating new technologies, they changed the shape of history.

Now such a time has come again.

We stand on the edge of a revolution that will hold a place of honor with the revolutions that preceded it. The computer age revolution, when used to its full advantage, will forever change the future. But first, we must become visionaries ourselves and entirely rethink the way we work and live.

Let's start by looking at where we've been so we can better see where we are going.

We will look back to those other revolutions and use the patterns revealed in them to allow us to better understand the current revolution—what we will call in this book, the Information Technology Revolution

Economists and growth theorists have used the term "General Purpose Technologies" (GPT) to define substantial or revolutionary technological breakthroughs.

One of these theorists, Richard Limpsey, grouped the innovations into 24 technologies. But, for our purposes, let's regroup them into only five and call each of the five a Revolution of its own:

The Agricultural Revolution:

Without this one, we would still be joining Og for his wild boar sushi and walking off our dinners by trudging, bag and baggage to the next hunting and gathering destination. The Agricultural Revolution found us learning about the sowing and harvesting of plants, how to domesticate animals so we always had a ready food supply, how to group together with other humans for security and helpful division of labor and how such early social structures taught us of the benefits of connecting with our fellow man, outside our immediate kinship circles.

The Engines Revolution:

Here we went from ox and plow to tractor and combine, freeing us from an inconstant food supply to requiring us to build silos to store our surplus; from shanks' mare and horse-drawn wagons to steamships and iron horses that could traverse a continent and tame any river; from weaving by hand to spinning jenny's and textile mills, from hewing logs to coal powered furnaces, from papyrus to paper, from hand made to factory produced, from powerless to powerful.

The Electrification Revolution:

"Early to bed, early to rise" was imposed on us by the inconvertible natural cycles of daylight and nighttime. Candles were precious and expensive and the night full of unseen terrors. A dark world, lit by tallow, tapers and oil, came blazingly to light during this revolution. Geniuses like Edison and Tesla, Marconi and Bell invented electric lights, telegraphs, telephones and wirelesses to change our gloomy insular world into a brightly lit global village. Sir Ambrose Fleming's vacuum tube, Michael Faraday's electric motor, transformer and generator and DE Forest's work with amplification not only greatly improved our present day lives, but paved the way for the next leap in technological advancement.

The Information Technology Revolution:

Here we now stand. When computer scientist Alan Turning first described the modern computer in 1936, he couldn't have known how ubiquitous these "computation machines" would become.

The early electromagnetic machines led to those with vacuum tubes, then to the first digital computers (used in WW II), then to machines that took up whole rooms and on to today's smartphones, Google Glass and Apple wristwatches which allow us to pack computing power in ever-smaller devices, and fashion ours truly as The Computer Age. The internet, the information highway that connects all of us no matter where we are in the world, created a new way of communicating, gathering and dissemination information and sharing knowledge in ways our forefathers would never have dreamed. Astonishing as the capabilities of this Information Technology Revolution are, I don't believe we have scratched the surface of the ways in which these technological strides could benefit us, changing the way we work and live, increasing our production, creating more value, easing our burdens, and improving the very our quality of our lives. These benefits and how we can achieve tem is the subject of this book.

There is one revolution yet to come, though we have seen the first stirrings of it in such things as the use of genetically modified organisms (GMO), crops and that is…

The Biotechnology Revolution:

Genetic modification isn't confined to crops alone. We stopped for a moment, as a race, and noted when Dolly the Sheep was cloned. We are now wrestling with the ethical implications of human cloning and its less incendiary cousin, genome mapping, gene therapies and stem cell use. We are developing bio-identical hormones and human ligaments and organs created on 3-D printers. Individual pharmaceuticals are being manufactured and target therapies to cure ills that have plagued us for centuries. As the aforementioned GMOs produce pesticide-resistant crops, allowing us to spray for insects without harming the plant, they may increase yield to help fight famine in perpetually stricken parts of the globe. We are on the brink on that Brave New World and our future will take on a shape we can't yet fully conceive, only glimpse.

With the fourth and fifth in the offing, let's more fully examine the three revolutions that have already taken place.

The Agricultural Revolution

"Nobody is qualified to become a statesman who is entirely ignorant of the problem of wheat."

—Socrates, Greek philosopher, 469 BC–399 BC

The first and probably most important technological revolution of mankind, which was responsible for the most incredible productivity gains, as we truly are what we eat (or don't eat), was the Agricultural Revolution, beginning with the Neolithic (Stone Age) Revolution. Thanks to technology, a fundamental change in the human way of life became possible. Humans evolved from hunter-gatherers to farmers, which happened at around 10,000 BC. Through the domestication of plants and livestock, humans were finally able to produce more food than they needed to consume immediately. This not only gave them the opportunity to store food for leaner times, but, since they could spend less effort hunting and gathering, they had more time on their hands— which inevitably led them to having more sex (some things haven't changed all that much) and producing more offspring.

Since our prehistoric ancestors could now grow the food where they were, instead of moving to where the food was, they stopped and put down roots, literally Permanent settlements started to appear, as did gardens and small farms. All these occurrences were preconditions for a significant jump in human development. People stopped wearing only skins and began weaving cloth. They wove baskets and made vessels. Things that could be traded were made and as social structures beyond the family or clan were formed, commerce took its first infant steps. Most importantly, people's brainpower increased as they were liberated from the constant necessity to focus all their attention on staying alive, and had time to think, ruminate and innovate.

All the knowledge we share today took root in

that most significant revolution, which for the first time in the world's history, gave a species the technology to gain more control of their food supply and allowed prehistoric man the leisure to start using his brainpower for other tasks.

Prior to The Agricultural Revolution, being able to assure the food supply took up almost all of humanity's attention. In comparison, today in the USA, the employment in agriculture is around 2% of the total employment. That frees up an enormous amount of working energy other purposes—a truly incredible productivity gain.

Credit for this moveable feast cannot be given to one single technological innovation. It was a string of innovations over thousands of years, which gradually helped to improve the output, storage, processing, and distribution, bringing us the benefits we know today. But everything started with the first domestication of plants and animals, forcing humans to plan, divide tasks, and use their brainpower in innovative ways. No other technological revolution has seen a similar productivity gain in the history of mankind.

The Engines Revolution

"Everything that can be invented has already been invented."

—Charles Duell, Commissioner for the
U.S. Patent Office, 1899

In the thousands of years after the beginning of

the Agricultural Revolution until the 19th century, many gradual improvements and innovations took place. These advancements included tool-making, expansion of arts, myriad social changes, and changes to the distribution of work, as well as the invention of capital markets and the introduction and capability of long-distance travel. Even though these would eventually bring significant benefits globally, the changes they wrought were mostly gradual. It can be argued that the true revolution began with the invention of James Watts' steam engine in 1775.

For the first time, engines freed production from relying on the input of man or animal muscle, water, or wind power that could produce the necessary force in almost any location at any time and at nearly any strength. This was a radical change that allowed for the Industrial Revolution, with its new production technologies and transportation enhancements in speed and its capacity to produce radical improvements in labor productivity. Just as the Agricultural Revolution freed mankind from using our energy largely to pursuing food, the Engine Revolution freed mankind from investing so much of his personal physical power to obtain a desired output. For the first time, physical power became less important than mental power.

As before with the Agricultural Revolution, the Engines Revolution, powered through increased access to fossil fuels like coal and iron ore, triggered a radical change in how many people across several continents would work and live. These countries would become known as "industrialized nations" and they would come to dominate world politics and affect worldwide commerce and nations' economic policies throughout the next century and beyond. In the lesser-developed nations, where the seismic change this revolution brought about was less rattling, eventually the benefits mankind derived from this revolution would be felt in all corners of the globe. Even today there is a strong correlation between economic growth and the input of energy, as measured in energy consumption. 2014 saw the first time in history, thanks to strides in energy efficiency technology, that growth increased while energy consumption actually decreased.

The Electrification Revolution

"When the Paris Exhibition [of 1878] closes, electric light will close with it and no more will be heard of it."

—Erasmus Wilson, Professor at Oxford University

When the lights came on, no one could conceive how electrification, started in the late 19th century in Great Britain and in the United States, would change the world. At first only a novelty or the stuff of World Fair exhibitions, the first applications were in the area of lighting, replacing gas or oil lamps. Soon electricity became the go-to technology for small local power needs in many areas, where large-scale engines were too expensive and the generated power too large for the needed usage. Mom-and-Pop businesses on Main Street, small factories in cities, schools, hospitals and farmhouses were soon able to get electricity and the world changed. In a sense, electrification was the democratization of the usage of power in business, small and large.

Through electrification and its equitable distribution an incredible technological and business revolution could take place. Even though electrification could be understood as part of the Engine Revolution, its impact was so far- reaching that it is widely considered as a revolution on its own.

Electrification gave us light, which revolutionized where and when we could work. It also gave us the telephone, which changed the way we could communicate. Refrigeration systems make it possible for us to store and transport food and live in hot and arid climates in comfort or generate heat in cold places. Radio, and eventually television, not only entertained us, but brought the news of the outside world into our homes and consciousness, turning our world into a true global village.

In the modern world, our lives depend so strongly on electricity that we are mostly unaware of its incomparable impact on our lives. Only when the power is out for a longer period, as we experience after natural catastrophes, like storms, hurricanes, and floods, do we become aware of all the things we do not have anymore and depend upon so much. One need only live through the power outages caused by hurricanes hitting my own Florida coast, to understand how life with becomes quickly unlivable. There is no air-conditioning as the temperature rises to its seasonal 100 degrees; no refrigeration so no ice can alleviate your thirst and the bottled water quickly turns hot enough to bathe in; no electrical pumps meaning all the standing water left behind becomes a thriving home for stinging insects and wandering snacks; no gasoline for sale to move your car (or family to higher ground); battery-powered radios are the only hope of getting news on the storm impact as cell phones can't be recharged and TV's don't work and the nights get very dark and dangerous with no houselights or street lights to guide you.

In economic terms, the impact is even more far-reaching. In 2002, Ayres and Warr published a research paper which states that the economic growth between 1900 and 1975 can be almost per-fectly explained by the increase in efficiency of en-ergy use—what they call *exergy*, or useful work, input. Until 1975, there was almost a perfect cor-relation. After 1975, growth was a little higher than can be explained by electrification, which they at-tribute to some positive impacts of information technology on growth[1].

---

[1]   Ayres, R. U., & Warr, B. (2002). *Two paradigms of production and*

Energy input and growth do appear to be directly correlated. In 2014 it was the first time growth increased while energy consumption decreased. This can probably be attributed to new energy efficiency uses.

The Information Technology Revolution

"I think there is a world market for maybe five computers."

—Thomas Watson, Chairman of IBM, 1943.

After freeing up time for tasks other than procuring food in the Agricultural Revolution, moving our focus from physical power to brain power in the Engines Revolution, and the democratization of technology in the Electrification Revolution, what was the next leap mankind made? It was the Information Technology Revolution and it was a revolution in the true sense of the word, overthrowing the way things had always been done (and done for a very long time) and replacing them with new tools, technologies and theories in what was a giant leap forward in almost all the ways we live and work.

We went from hand-computing methods like the abacus, the slide rule and the comptometer to machines that did such computations for us and did so faster and more accurately. From using geometry to plot a submarine's missile track and decoding cryptography in World War II to directing the
growth. INSEAD: Fontainbleau, France.

Space Shuttle's docking procedures and crunching the thousands of numbers necessary for the proper functioning of the Large Hadron Collider, we have made mind-blowing gains in the development of our technology. The internet alone, wherein millions of people, all across the globe, can communicate instantly, sharing data, photos, videos and information that can not only transform industry and our social connections, but can also literally topple governments and change world order, as was seen during the Arab Spring. Such powerful technology surely has made great inroads in upping our productivity and profits, hasn't it?

No.

Though there is a lot of flash and dazzle in this ability to be in constant and nearly instantaneous touch with practically everyone else in the world, from a Maasai tribesman to a scientist stationed in Antarctica, the truth is that, when it comes to productivity gains, this Information Technology Revolution seems to be "all hat and no cattle."

All previous technology revolutions brought long-lasting productivity gains, but this has not happened with the Information Technology Revolution.

Robert M. Solow, a renowned US economist, wrote, "We can see the computers everywhere, *except* in the productivity statistics."

Productivity growth has actually slowed over the last decades and does not seem to be picking up.

Robert J. Gordon, <u>Stanley G. Harris</u> Professor of the Social Sciences at <u>Northwestern University</u> sets forth some obvious improvements in labor productivity that occurred because of information technology in the 1970s and 1980s. But since then, innovation has mainly occurred in the area of entertainment and the use of communication devices, with only limited impact on labor productivity or improvements in our standard of living.

Figure 1 from Gordon shows a significant growth increase in the beginning of the 20th century, mainly thanks to the previous revolutions and a steep drop in the last decades.

Growth in Real GDP per year

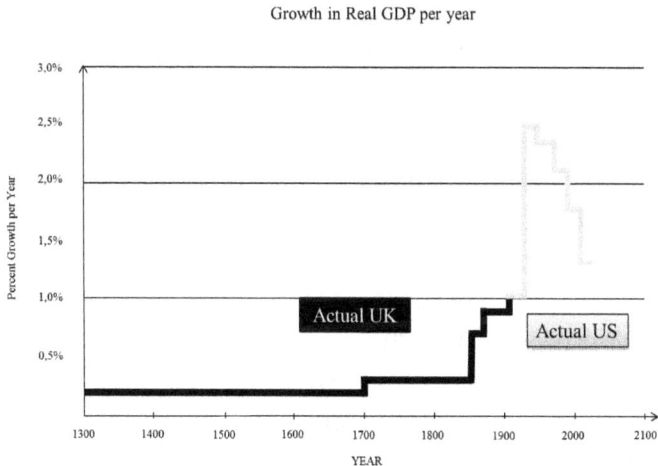

Figure 1: Source: Robert J. Gordon, "Is U.S. Economic Growth Over?" Northwestern University and CEPR, 2012

Gordon argues that the 150 years of US output per capita growth is basically a once-in-a-lifetime windfall coming from the different technology revolutions in the past, which can only happen once and will not happen again. The invention of running water and plumbing, for example, which freed up an enormous amount of household work time, has brought substantial productivity gains over a long period. Likewise we increased our energy efficiency through the adaption of compact fluorescent (CF) bulbs and LED lights make even further strides, but we all have gotten most of the benefit we will get from the technology of the electric light. We can move to variable speed air-conditioners, but the miracle of taming unlivable temperature conditions has now been accomplished. These gains have now been achieved—basically everybody in the USA benefits from those inventions—and looking forward, they will not yield any additional growth.

Like water technology, Gordon argues there are no other fields of technologic advances that are still to be discovered that could give similar growth statistics for the future. He believes that once this period is over (which will be soon), growth will be reduced to long-term growth similar to what the world saw before the technological revolutions in the 17th century.

Furthermore, the growth numbers for the last decades would have to be revised downward due to the "borrowed" growth foisted upon future generations. One driver for growth was not real economic growth, but growth acquired through debt. Public debt in the last three decades increased more than fivefold (see the following graph). One day this debt has to be repaid, having negative impacts on growth. Taking into effect the growth impact of such borrowed funds, the growth ratio in the last three decades was smaller still.

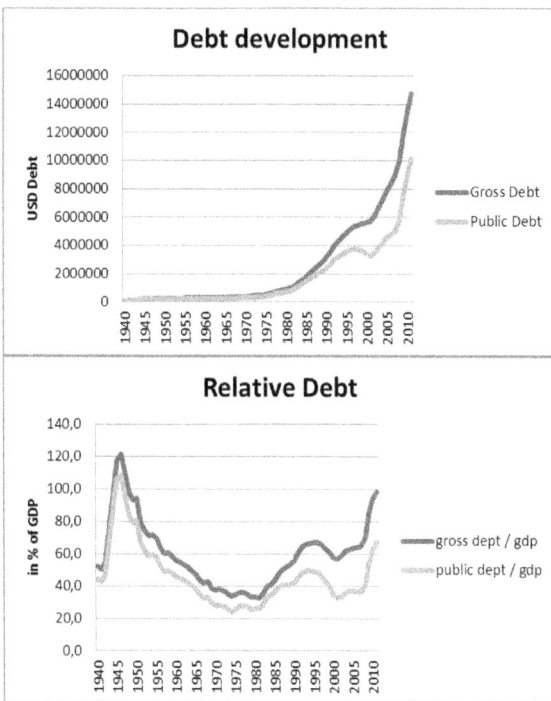

Figure 2: U.S. Debt Development: Source: Wikipedia

But is such a grim growth scenario set in stone? Can nothing be done to raise the temperature on future growth and turn it from a bed of slumbering coals, threatening to flicker out, to a blazing inferno, destined to set future economic growth on fire?

I think the answer is right before us now. The information technology we possess absolutely has the potential to set growth in the future on fire—all we have to do is use the matches we are holding.

Chad Syverson, Professor of Economics at the University of Chicago, compared the labor productivity development between electrification in 1890 and the dawn of information technology in 1970 and the productivity growth since then (see Figure 3). If the Information Technology Revolution follows the curve of the Electrification Revolution, (as it has done for the last 40 years), then the big productivity gains are still ahead of us. There are good reasons why this should be true:

US labor productivity growth after Electrification (1890)
vs.
US labor productivity growth after Information Technology (1970)

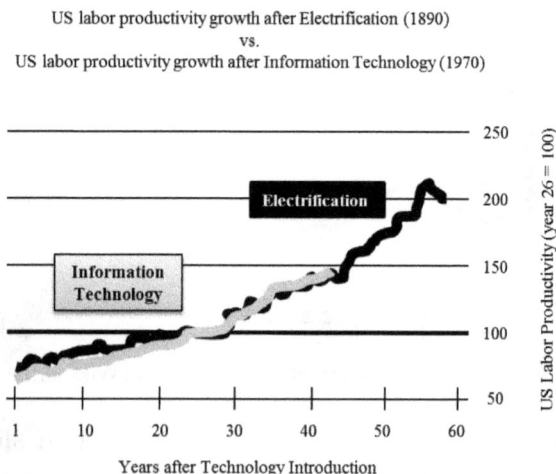

Figure 3: Productivity after Electrification and Information Technology, Source: The Economist: "Has the ideas machine broken down?" January 2013

All historic technology revolutions have taken a long time from when they began, through their full implementation when their value could spread to the whole society.

The Agricultural Revolution took thousands of years until mankind would widely adopt the new technologies and all could benefit from its use. From the time the first group of humans domesticated plants and animals until they created a widespread application of that technology, thousands of years had passed. The overall growth in productivity was relatively small and spread out over a long time.

The Engines Revolution had a more immediate impact, but it was still probably 100 years long until its peak growth impact.

The Electrification Revolution was still much faster, but overall almost 80 years passed until all the benefits were in place and, even at that, the first 30 years after the adoption of electrification passed virtually unnoticed in terms of factory productivity. In the beginning, managers replaced old technology (steam engines) with new technology (motors), but processes, organization and company culture would remain the same. It would take a new generation of managers to unlock the full potential, completely changing the way businesses worked.

Information technology has been around for about 40 years and in office automation, big changes have happened. But in general, our businesses, employees, and managers still work in a similar way as they did before information technology arrived. We are stuck in a time warp, saddled with outmoded ways of doing things; quite literally constrained by thinking entirely "in the box" when what we need to do is rip the box apart at the seams. The big productivity gains will come once businesses and public organizations do more than just occasionally "push the envelope", but rather change fundamentally to take full advantage of the new possibilities.

Our thinking and many of our methods are stuck in organizational and structural concepts from yesteryear. During the Industrial Revolution, the needs of machines dictated what the men around them needed to do to get work completed successfully. But in our present time, it will take a new generation of entrepreneurs, the companies they found and the managers they employ to create the fundamental changes that must be made for us to continue forward into a bright and productive future.

What types of changes are required and how businesses can best implement these changes is what I discuss in detail further along in this book. Please keep reading.

The Second Half of the Chessboard

This idea is based on an ancient story about the inventor of the chessboard. It is said that when the inventor showed his game to the king, the latter liked it so much, that he asked the inventor to tell him the price for his invention. He told the king to give him one rice grain for the first square and always double that amount for the next squares (two in the second, four in the third, etc.) until the last square of the board. The king readily agreed, thinking it to be a low price and had his treasurer pay him the price. Once the treasurer calculated the price, to the king's surprise, the amount of rice he was supposed to pay was much larger that all the treasures he had (it would be about 1,000 times the global rice production in 2010).

Ray Kurzweil, an American inventor, entrepreneur, and futurist, applied this idea to technology, with the base idea that an exponentially growing factor can have significant economic impact when it reaches a certain size (the "second half of the chessboard").

Revolutionary technologies behave in this way. The first telephone had no impact at all, beyond astounding those present at the first call when Alexander Graham Bell asked his assistant, Mr. Watson to come in the room.

With the second telephone installed, a one-to-one connection could be established between people (a vast improvement over that first summons Bell made to Watson) and the first verbal communication between two individuals over a distance happened—making the world a much smaller place.

With every new square (double the number of telephone lines installed), the benefit grew exponentially. Today almost any human being can call any other human being, bringing mankind much closer together. Looking at the Information Technology Revolution, many new technologies and applications have been discovered and put in play, but just as Kurzweil noted, with every move on the chessboard, the possibilities of these technologies and applications and their impact double.

For example, when Ford developed the Model T automobile he revolutionized personal mobility. We have happily adopted this now indispensable technology and used it for more than 100 years, yet it is only now that we are moving another space on the board regarding our automobiles. We have finally developed a driverless car by bringing together technological information from many different areas –enhanced automotive parts, global positioning units, traffic cams, road sensors, computerized imaging—to make an extraordinary advance, one that, when widely adopted, will allow for enormous productivity gains. The individual technologies that came together to allow for this advancement have all existed for some time independently. It is in their combination wherein the "magic." lies

It isn't, of course, magic that provides us with the impetus necessary to make such advancement. It is the computer power able to process huge amounts of information very quickly which opens up new and unexpected possibilities.

In their book *Race Against The Machine*[2], Brynjolfsson and McAfee argue that in 2006, information technology moved into the second half of the chessboard, and would continue moving one square ahead every 18 months. This is a restatement of 'Moore's Law', first posited by Intel and Fairchild Semiconductor co-founder Gordon E. Moore in 1965 with regards to the doubling of physical component counts on integrated circuits. But even as growth of transistor counts and clock speed of physical processors has slowed in the past decade from the 18-month doubling pace Moore envisioned, information technology has benefited and will continue to benefit from the sheer prevalence of computing devices and their increasing interconnectedness.

There are indications that such acceleration is already taking place. Today, your cell phone has more computing power than all of NASA had in 1969, when we placed a man on the moon. The head of a pin has room now for billions of transistors (without even evicting a legion of angels). Drones can fight a war. Robots can build a car. The detailed digital information provided by Cochlear implants can make the deaf hear and computer-guided laser technology can make the blind see.

---

[2] Brynjolfsson, Erick and Andrew McAfee (2012). *Race Against The Machine: How the Digital Revolution is Accelerating Innovation, Driving Productivity, and Irreversibly Transforming Employment and the Economy*. Digital Frontier Press.

Things are speeding up and the growth, I believe, is unstoppable.

The Three Stages of the Information Technology Revolution

But, like with every new idea, the adoption of a concept or technology is not universal from Day One. The first level of adoption normally happens where impact is highest and the applications are the most obvious. This is called the "low-hanging fruit". In the Information Technology Revolution, the "fruit" has mainly been harvested in the area of office automation used to replace repetitive human administrative work by information technology. As a consequence, we implement computer systems as part of the administrative areas of companies, once again using those same time-worn processes and structures as we did since the 18th Century. We didn't rethink the administrative processes themselves, just automated many of the same processes that were developed during the Industrial Revolution, further setting in amber these administrative dinosaurs.

The second stage was in the consumer arenas of gadgets and entertainment. This wave has mainly been driven by young entrepreneurs building apps, games, tools, and gadgets. Many have been used to amuse or address a small-scale specific need of their own (while I might download the "no-Kardashian" app myself, I'm not sure it adds much to productivity or human evolution.)

The third and last stage will be to value the information available from the current revolution and use it to change the way business, and society itself, is organized—to create what I call a *human-centric* organization. I'll discuss these three stages further in the next chapter.

Summary: The History of Technology Revolutions

To better understand the Information Technology Revolution, we have to gain some distance to be able to see the big picture; a historic perspective will give us the required clarity.

Just as Og learned how to make use of tools and new technology to move from being a hunter/gatherer; as Frick learned to smelt steel ties the Iron horses used to span the continent; as Texas wildcatters found how to drill the black gold from the ground to fuel Mr. Ford's horseless carriage, as Edison learned to power the globe; as Bell learned to make the world talk, as IBM's Bill Lowe developed the first PC—so we, too, must stand on the shoulders of those who went before us. We must milk the Information Technology Revolution for all it can give us. We mustn't stop with such tools as the internet, smart phones, cloud computing or ERP and CAD Systems, but continue to innovate and build upon those technologies. To do so, we must literally overthrow the status quo. We can't continue to do "business as usual". It must be "business as unusual" and it must shake the very foundations of how not only offices, corporations and factories are run, but schools, hospitals and social interactions as well. Concepts of organization, processes and structure that served us so well in prior decades now serve as stumbling blocks hindering our ability to make the next leap forward.

It is time for us to become revolutionaries.

CHAPTER TWO

STAGESOFTHEINFORMATION TECHNOLOGYREVOLUTION

"Again, you can't connect the dots looking forward; you can only connect them looking backwards. So you have to trust that the dots will somehow connect in your future. You have to trust in something—your gut, destiny, life, karma, whatever. This approach has never let me down, and it has made all the difference in my life."

—Steve Jobs (1955–2011), co-founder of Apple Inc.

Stage 1 (1970–2000): Low-Hanging Fruit - The Office Automation Stage

Every change has a catalyst; every fire a spark and the match that lit the world-changing bomb that became the Information Technology Revolution was the invention of the computer. The explosion it precipitated blew up business as we knew it and things were never the same again.

Computers were around for quite some time before they had much of an impact beyond specific niche applications. The first computer was built in 1936 by German engineer Konrad Zuse, but the applications were very limited, mostly for specific calculation tasks. In the 1950s, the first commercial computers came on the market, but it took until the 1970s, and the invention of memory chips, microprocessors, floppy disks, and networking, that the Information Technology Era had begun and with it, how we conducted business changed forever.

The first word processors freed us from the clacking of typewriters; digital printers did away with carbon paper and retired all the mimeograph machines (and with them, purple ink-stained fingers) and spreadsheets tracked everything from mountains of incoming data to profit-and-loss statements with an ease never matched by any accountant's hand-written ledger.

The tipping point was soon reached and we tumbled, headlong, into the sea of computing power available for both business and personal use that had the potential to drown us in information, but instead challenged us to grab the rope, climb on up and harness the vast potential of the Information Technology Revolution and make it work for us. We rose to the challenge and soon applications were springing up almost faster than we could assimilate them. The Information Technology Revolution was underway.

Prior to the 1970s, computers were just machines designed for specific tasks. Those tasks would run on standalone computers with limited capabilities and the information they generated would be local information for local use. But in the 1970s, we saw the introduction of networking and the subsequent integration of computers along with the introduction of standard software products. Suddenly a single point-of-use technology became available not only to the huge corporation, but the small business, as well as the entrepreneur burning the midnight oil alone at his dining room table, dreaming of how to start his own company. What we think of as The Computer Age was in its infancy and like fearful new parents, every hiccup and cough raised alarms. Many of us were concerned about this new technology and worried about how it would transform our world. Would the machines dictate the way we had to work? What is we couldn't understand or learn what would now be expected of us? Perhaps this new technology might take our jobs from us entirely? But each of us felt an undercurrent also, felt a surge of excitement about the potential this new technology might open for us. A brave new world beckoned and we watched the technology take its baby steps with both trepidation and anticipation.

Soon the new technology was making invaluable contributions to science, medicine and academia, allowing researchers, scientists and teachers to save thousands of hours and make greater strides in their work (and gaining the potential to share those strides easily and globally) than ever before in history. In smaller, but in the end, no less important ways, the new technology was forever changing the face of business. The hundreds of simple, repetitive but vital office tasks like invoicing, bookkeeping, account management, master data management, reservation systems, production planning, and supply chain management, were automated. Strong efficiency gains were made in transactional work and a human's brainpower was being replaced by programmable computers that did a quicker, better job processing information with fewer mistakes. Machines basically replaced human in many tasks and this was a good thing. The impact this had on the economy in general was that repetitive white collar jobs became obsolete and could be performed by technology, while many new technology jobs were created to develop and implement that technology. The overall productivity gain out of that period is questionable; however an important shift from white collar clerks to technology jobs took place. Still, in this embryonic phase of the Information Technology Revolution, no one yet had the foresight to see that the computer and its application would soon have the ability to reconfigure the way in which business was done forever—to change the entire definition of "work" in the future.

The way a company works, and how an employee is supposed to complete a task for the company, has not fundamentally changed, despite the introduction of new technology in businesses. Companies might employ fewer administrative staff today, and work has in some ways become more demanding, but the general concept of defining work, processes, and distribution of labor, evaluation of employees, organization, and hierarchy hasn't changed that much since the Industrial Revolution.

Smelting machines and factory production lines once dictated the rhythm of work and now Enterprise Resource Planning (ERP) business management software sets the pace, but only is rare cases have humans been freed from their established work tasks to allow their ever-evolving brains to be free to create, innovate and produce—creating value for their companies in ways now only glimpsed through a glass darkly. Technology offers the tools to break the shackles of the past and catapult business into a productive and fascinating future. We need only tap its potential.

Stage 2 (1990–2020): Internet, Gadgets, and Entertainment: The Consumer Stage

"Television won't be able to hold on to any market it captures after the first six months. People will soon get tired of staring at a plywood box every night."

—Darryl Zanuck, 20th Century Fox, 1946.

In 1982, the Commodore 64 model computer was introduced. Soon millions of people were lugging the machine home, making it the single highest-selling computer model of all time and earning it a place in *The Guinness Book of World Records*. This Model T of computers brought technology into the living room where consumers eagerly watching the green scale monochromatic screen, with its blinking cursor and welcome "ready" command, to play *Pitfall!* and *Flight Simulator II* for hours on end. Many fathers and sons bonded over such experiences and a tech-savvy group of teenagers was born.

These same teens, who fell in love with the games, went on to take their devotion into the workplace and, making use of the technology they first learned playing those games, produced today's "internet economy" and went on to found such companies as Amazon (1994), eBay (1995), and Google (1998). These companies in turn had, as their early users, the people who would go on to found Facebook (2004), Twitter (2006), Dropbox (2007) and Instagram (2010).

One thing all these blazingly successful companies share is that they were all founded by business neophytes. Their founders were all in their twenties, often dreaming up their business idea in a college dorm room to solve a problem they were experiencing personally. Not since the beginning of the Industrial Revolution has it been possible for startup companies to be envisioned and begun by people with virtually no business experiences. Yet these young people developed breakthrough technologies, making use of the new information technology, and had those companies grow into global players almost immediately.

The more established IT companies like Nintendo (founded in 1889), IBM (1911), Samsung (1938), Hewlett-Packard (1939), Sony (1946), SAP (1972), Microsoft (1975), and Oracle (1977), have either focused on the consumer or on traditional information technology products and services. Such companies have brought large productivity gains to their customers, but only at great cost and often their success can be traced to their strong market position (brand strength) and not through their innovations or use of revolutionary technologies. They no longer invent things themselves, but rather buy innovative products or entire innovative companies. They have maintained their level of success and market share through their focus on sales of their existing technologies and by their brand strength, established through decades of marketing effort.

Neither of those two groups has brought any new technology to the market, nor any advances that have substantially increased productivity in the marketplace. It can be argued that these companies that they have brought significant *noneconomic* benefits to society, through new forms of entertainment and social interaction, but the overall economic benefit, as measured by economists is negligible and have come about despite new technologies and often cementing the old ways into their dealings with the company's processes and their customers.

Unlike what we saw at the beginning of the Industrial Revolution, where new technologies (like automobiles), led to the opening of huge factories with hundreds of thousands of employees, companies like Twitter (with 1,000 employees) or even Facebook (with nearly 5,000 employees) have had almost no impact on overall employment numbers, even though they have market valuations beyond companies with hundreds of times the employees. Facebook's Market Cap in April 2013 of $61 billion, with its 1,000 employees, stands in stark contrast to GM's Market Cap during the same period. With 213,000 employees, GM's cap was only $40 billion. Technology, in this instance, made market valuations rise, yet reduced the needed workforce dramatically. The preceding revolutions, (Agricultural and Industrial) increased productivity, but also intrinsically changed the way companies worked and the way business was conducted. I feel certain that this Information Technology Revolution, which has just begun, will have the same transformative power on today's companies and ways of doing business—but it hasn't yet.

When we look hard at today's business environment, we see that, for all the fascinating new technologies and gadgets of the last 20 years, none of them have truly overturned the way companies are run or business is done in the way one might expect of technology with such revolutionary capacity.

After the first wave of information technology innovation and productivity gains, once that low-hanging fruit has been picked, their lasting impact on business has been marginal, even though they have made a big splash in the pool of personal communication, gaming, entertainment, access to information, and opinion building.

Except for the presence of electricity and some slight change in fashion, if you had seen me attending university 20 years ago, you would see much the same scene as if I were in that classroom in 1896 as opposed to 1986. I sat there unmoving, listened to my professor's lecture, took notes on paper, read books, visited the library, researched case studies and fed the information I received back to my teachers via papers, quizzes, tests and by answering their questions in class. This rote process verified that I understood the material the professor had been trying to teach me and was therefore worthy of a degree.

Today's students sit in a classroom (or an online virtual classroom), listen to a professor, take notes on their laptop, tablet or portable device; read books (sometimes on a Kindle or Nook), visit the library, research case studies (mostly online) and feed the information back to their teachers in the form of papers (word processed and printed), quizzes and tests (rarely online for security purposes) and by answering questions in class.

Aside from how the information is accessed and shared, the way subjects are taught today differs very little from the way in which things were taught before the Information Technology Revolution began.

Yet that student, the second class is out, will use Foursquare to tell all his friends where he'll meet them; take a Snapchat of himself and someone he ran into on the quad, edit it to use a special filter, add a caption and send it out to another group of friends; use SoundHound to listen to the music he hears from a nearby laptop, figure out the song, download an MP3 on iTunes of it directly to his phone and be listening to it with a minute. He can (illegally) download a first run movie to watch tonight while appearing as though he is in Halstead Sweden to avoid paying fees; hookup with a date for the night on Tinder and bring up 17 sites to cut and paste research for his homework assignment paper, complete with illustrative photos from Dreamstime or permission-free from Google Images. He can keep up with his avatar on World of Warhammer, a game he is playing with cyber friends in Japan and Australia and talk to his mom in a separate window via Google chat or Skype on his laptop all before he gets back to his dorm room (where he will ask for money to be sent to his on-line PayPal account) and yet none of the individualized technologies available today have been put to use in educating the next generation. Technology has yet to be put to use to customize a student's education.

How do we use technology in the office today? After graduation, my first employer, (a Swiss technology company active in a variety of industrial fields, like food packaging machines, trains, and arms), was just implementing a new Enterprise Resource Planning (ERP) system, including corporate e-mail and 3D CAD systems, The company still had an internal postal service (phased out within two years), and every executive still had a "secretary" (most of whom morphed into "assistants" within a few years). Aside from those few changes, the way the company works today, in developing technology, executing production, administrating the company, and organizing sales is still the same as when I joined the company more than two decades ago.

Or let's look at other fields like public services, healthcare and retail. In none of those industries has information technology of the last 20 years had much impact in the way things are done, (the exception being the near-death of the brick-and-mortar store now that much merchandise is purchased over the internet. But, even online, buyers still put their merchandise in a "cart" and still go to "checkout" to purchase the items). Retailers that are still frequented in person, like grocery stores, still have the cashier scan a barcode on the products (a technology introduced in 1972).

Except in major metropolitan areas (and even

there, too often), you must send a paper check in the mail to pay your water bill. You still vote using a punch card machine (despite the hanging chad scandals of elections passed). Your social security card is still paper and the US Postal Service still limps along.

Your doctor's office still has you fill out sheet after sheet of paper on a clipboard detailing your family history and, should you change doctors or move, you must fill out paper permission slips to have your medical records faxed to your new doctor's office. Despite some feints at "patient portals", where you can ask for refills or leave a question for the doctor, this is often more for their convenience than their patients and you will still get a paper bill (or several, if you are late in paying.)

And in most of our daily jobs, we still work in an office, store, or factory from 8 am to 5 pm, with or without a lunch break, and we basically still get the same job done in the same way as did our parents or even grand and great grandparents.

Our workplaces look more modern and we have devices like smartphones and laptops, which give us constant access to our communication tools (and give everyone from clients to our bosses, 24-hour access to us.) Despite the upscale cubicles and the constant online presence, the actual way we get the job done is the same as it has been for decades.

Why has so little changed? The answer lies in the analogy that moving anything within a bureaucracy is like reversing direction on a cruise ship, as opposed to a kayak. One can turn on a dime; the other moves its creaky old bulk very slowly.

There is, of course, another dimension to the answer. Change always comes slowly at the macro level of a company, the executive branch (where such decisions are made). When the question is asked, "Why do we do things this way?" the answer is, "That's the way we've always done it". Not too deeply hidden in that answer is a fact of human nature: Why would The Powers That Be wish to change that which made them The Powers That Be? Innovation would upset the status quo and they *are* the status quo. To change might be planning their own funeral.

Another reason for the lack of responsiveness to change in modern businesses, despite the advent of new technology, is that those who understand the technology make use of it strictly as consumers, not taking that one further leap of logic by apply it to improving their work environment or the company for which they work sees the new technology as something they should only sell to other companies—thus the fact that the true IT behemoths, like HP and IBM themselves haven't made us of the new technology to fundamentally change their corporate culture.

So the question remains: Why has the majority of value creation not taken advantage of those new technologies in more fundamental ways?

Stage 3 (2010–2040): The Online Generation: Business and Knowledge Revolution

"It's a dangerous business, Frodo, going out your door. You step onto the road, and if you don't keep your feet, there's no knowing where you might be swept off to."

— J.R.R. Tolkien, *The Lord of the Rings*

Those recent IT entrepreneurs, like Steve Jobs, who started experimenting with those first personal computers to come up with business ideas, had a different experience than the digital natives of the current generation.

Infants now have online lullabies sung to them. Toddlers are given tablets to entertain themselves. Elementary school students take their smartphone to school and have folders full of their own apps. Junior High schools kids, a recent study discovered[3], send over 60 texts a day to their friends and try to pry a High School student off of their phone or tablet, (where they are constantly using Instagram, Twitter, Facebook, Snapchat, Tumblr and its cooler impersonators like Whisper and Kik) and it's as though you amputated their limb.

Prospective sweethearts don't ask the object of

[3] Samakow, J. (2012, March 19). *Teen Texting: New Report Shows They Send 60 Texts A Day*. Retrieved February 7, 2016 from The Huffington Post: http://www.huffingtonpost.com/2012/03/19/texting-and-teens_n_1365650.html

their affection out on a date—they text the question. Invitations no longer arrive in the mail—Evites are sent, asking for emailed RSVPs. No one sits and flips through a photo album anymore. Photos are shared instantly while the vacationer is still on the beach. I actually know a young mother who tweeted and posted photos on Facebook of her labor with her first child while she was experiencing it!

Nothing is private, all is public, and everything is immediate.

Michel Serres, a French philosopher, compared the changes communication has recently undergone to the change when mankind moved from solely speaking, to writing, as a form of communication (6,000 years ago) and then from handwriting copies of publications to printing (600 years ago). He found that the current change in the way we access knowledge and communicate with one another is another society-altering occurrence, comparable in magnitude to the advent of both written and printed communication, with the same far-reaching impacts to politics, the economy, and our society as a whole as those that went before it.

Let's put the social changes of the new generation into perspective with the other two great changes in the way we humans communicate: communication revolutions:

The Written Word

Thanks to The Agricultural Revolution, mankind began to settle down, build communities, and develop trade. As this process expanded and more complex social structures and economic systems evolved, we discovered that our oral tradition of handing down songs, stories and the history or our peoples didn't accommodate everything for which there needed to be a record kept—as, for example, would be required for trade goods transactions. This need to reliably transmit information and keep records led to the development of the written word. This new technology allowed for a fundamental change in society (governance and law), economy (trade), and the transfer of knowledge, which allowed for society to evolve.

Naturally, as with all tools of power, reading and writing were at first reserved for only a small group of privileged people. Most people did not learn to read or write (and were duly cheated often, we might imagine.)

Printing is Introduced

Until the invention of the printing press, every text had to be hand written by the specialists, the literate ones, in an expensive and time-consuming process. With Gutenberg's printing press, the written word could suddenly be reproduced on a massive scale.

Before the development of the printing press in

the 14th century, a total of 3 million books had been produced in Europe. By the 16th century, this had already grown to 200 million books and in the 18th century to 1 billion books. This was a hundredfold increase in the availability of books, allowing for a spread of knowledge unequaled in history.

As more people became literate and able to write, new ideas were shared, which led directly to The Enlightenment; more (often passionate) participation in self-governing, which spawned such historical convulsions as The French and American Revolutions; as well as new interpretations of religion, creation of compulsory schooling and economic booms.

The printing press was the Great Equalizer taking the power of knowledge out of the hands of a few privileged people in government, religion and academia and putting it into the hands of the wider public.

Communication Goes Online

The printed word, while eventually available to almost everybody, was still a top-down technology when it came to transmitting knowledge, ideas, and opinions.

The online revolution is a much more accessible. Via networks, physical and digital, knowledge is shared worldwide virtually instantaneously. Those who once stood as gatekeepers—politicians and government officials, academics and intelligentsia, publishers and media, are rapidly losing influence in a world where almost all knowledge is available to almost all people, no matter their education, age, political persuasion or geographical location. Within minutes, virtually anybody's tweet, blog, Facebook post, instant message or YouTube video can be read or seen, get shared, go viral and influence the opinions and actions of millions of people worldwide.

The ramifications of such instantly and democratically shared information are astounding; as was witnessed in the recent Arab Spring demonstrations. Photos and videos shared from the scene and spread to like-minded people throughout the region, literally toppled governments.

From the leaking of a waiter's secretly recorded video ending the campaign of Republican presidential candidate Mitt Romney, to a nine-year-old California schoolgirl posting daily photos protesting her school's lunch selections which went viral and predicated a complete change in a school systems' nutritional program, the power of online communication is indisputable.

The medium also has reworked not only what is information is shared between people, but *how* it is shared—a distinction that affects education in profound ways.

American economist Tyler Cowen expressed, "Browsing the Web has, on average, a higher educational value than watching TV or many of the older ways of 'wasting time.' People can spend their time, where they see individual fulfillment, and more than ever try to put their real talents to use, instead of the work most accessible to them."

Such I believe will be the future of work.

The people who make up the online generation truly have the ability to reinvent themselves without being hindered by lack of educational opportunity, socio-economic class or even geographical location. The playing field is being leveled whether you are from Mumbai, Mombasa or Minneapolis.

Educational researcher Dr. Sugata Mitra's "Hole in the Wall" experiments have shown that, in the absence of supervision or formal teaching, children can teach themselves and each other.

In 1999, Mitra and his colleagues dug a hole in a wall bordering an urban slum in New Delhi, installed an Internet-connected PC and left it there. What they saw was kids playing around with the computer, and in the process learning how to use it, how to go online, and teaching each other. The "Hole in the Wall" project demonstrates that an environment that stimulates curiosity can cause learning through self-instruction and peer-shared knowledge. Mitra, who's now a professor of educational technology at Newcastle University, calls it "minimally invasive education."

"In nine months, a group of children left alone with a computer — in any language — would reach the same standard as an office secretary in the West," said Mitra[4].

---

[4] *How Much Can Children Teach Themselves*. (2015, September 4). Retrieved July 5, 2015 from NPR TED Radio Hour: http://www.npr.org/2013/06/21/179015266/how-much-can-children-teach-themselves

Such is the power of the Information Technology Revolution.

Authors Eric Schmidt and Jared Cohen co-authored a book "The New Digital Age: Transforming Nations, Businesses And Our Lives," the subject of which is what the online generation will expect from their world and what that could mean for government, work, and the changes to them in the form of revolutions, terrorism and conflict. They argue that online technology will alter the way states (repressive or democratic) and citizens interact, as well as how the imposition of surveillance and other repression will likely eventually leading to future revolutions.

Part of their argument about surveillance was proven true in the 2013 NSA scandal surrounding Edward Snowden, which laid bare, how much information the State (even a democratic State like the United States) gathers from friends and foes in the name of security.

The borderline between the security of the individual and their right to the protection of their personal information versus the rights of the State to protect the sanctity of information it deems too dangerous to release publically will be a line much more difficult to draw in the future.

The technology-immersed children growing up today will see the world differently and interact with it and each other in ways we can't yet imagine. What we do know is that because of the Information Technology Revolution, they will have different expectations of politics, education, leisure, geo-politics and work than any previous generation.

This generation will reshape the way we do business and the way we create value in new and unexpected ways. As we have seen in the first wave of adapters to the Computer Age, it is not the first generation after the new technology becomes available that reaps the greatest benefits; it is the second generation, the one who needn't overcome old, ingrained ways of thinking. This generation, the digital native, for whom the "new" technology is no longer new, but Mothers Milk to them, they are the ones who can use the technology as a springboard to recreate their environment—business and in all other ways.

When it comes to value creation, this means that the new online generation is open to change the way businesses and services are run to take full advantage of the potential offered by the Information Technology Revolution as no generation before them has been.

What we have seen so far from the Information Technology Revolution is truly only a glimpse of the tip of a very large iceberg. The part we've yet to see, below the waterline, will change the world.

CHAPTER THREE

IFYOUAREN'TPARTOFTHE
SOLUTION...

*"We cannot solve our problems with the same thinking
we used when we created them."*

— Albert Einstein (1879–1955), Nobel Prize
winner for Physics

The Newtonian Law about an object in motion
staying in motion just as well may apply to
how we view work. If it ain't (totally) broke, don't
fix it. We just keep on keeping on doing things the
way they have long been done, until we are forced
to make a change.

Thus, when the Agricultural Revolution came
along, and we laid down the hand-plow, allowing
the oxen to become the dumb animals in our place,
the division of labor changed and the process by
which we sowed and reaped become more sophisticated.

When The Industrial Revolution began, we
changed things again. Work became mechanized

and production increased exponentially, but in both these instances one thing did not change: The organization of work was dictated by external forces. If it was raining hard, the crops didn't get planted for fear the seed would wash away. If the machine needed lubrication, work stopped until the axle grease was applied. The farm work revolved around the weather; factory work around the machine. The needs of the humans operating within both of these systems were secondary. He might as well have been just another "cog in the machine."

That type of thinking is with us still and it affects how modern enterprises are run and influences students of management and management theory to this day, hindering us from taking full advantage of the advances made possible by the Information Technology Revolution.

Since we have to name it to claim it and claim it to change it, let's examine the roots of what passes for modern business theory and why we are so resistant to change.

Making Work Tougher

"Most of what we call management consists of making it difficult for people to get their work done."

—Peter Drucker (1909–2005), leading management consultant, educator, and author

Taylorism/Scientific Management

When the Engines Revolution (which led to the Industrial Revolution) began, an entrepreneur's most important investments were the tools and machines necessary to manufacture whatever he was manufacturing.

Take, for example, England's Matthew Murray, who, in 1795, became one of the world's finest producers of textile machinery, steam engines and locomotives. His Round Foundry developed to become one of the world's first specialist engineering foundries. The manufactory was equipped with three steam engines for driving the machine tools. After manufacture the parts were assembled in a testing department, and when run-in and tested the engines were dis-assembled for packing and dispatch. The firm was renowned for the elegant design of their engines, and the quality of manufacture. They were pioneers of all-metal construction and the development of portable engines - engines that could be taken to pieces and easily moved to another location.

Such advances made mass production possible and, without doubt, moved mankind along the rails of progress in a way that would change the world, but the workers themselves, who did the backbreaking work in foundry and factory to make these marvels possible were still low-skilled, poorly paid and eminently replaceable.

In 1881, Frederick Taylor introduced time study

into American manufacturing, leading to this subsequent theory of management science that would come to be known as "Taylorism". Essentially, Taylor suggested that production efficiency in a shop or factory could be greatly enhanced by close observation of the individual worker and elimination of waste time and motion in his operation.

While studying the workflows in such industrial environments, Taylor discovered that management's view of the worker was to see him as just a piece of a machine, or worse, as the same dumb farm animal which he had been viewed as for the preceding centuries—one that needed as much prodding and poking to work as that ox did to drag a plow.

Taylor's theories helped bring into being efficiency measures and rules about how exactly a worker was to do his job. Implementation of these measures and rules meant that the worker had to follow established protocols. Failure to follow the rules (or inability to keep up) meant the worker was out and another immediately took his place. The process, not the person, was the most important thing. Nothing could stand in the way of progress in that most progressive age. True, this helped reduce cost, increase efficiency and appeared to be (at the time) the only way to guarantee the success of mass production, but it did reduce humans to being only one factor, and not the most important factor at that, in achieving maximum output.

The 1936 movie *Modern Times* by Charlie Chaplin is a great example of that production philosophy at work.

In the film, Chaplin's iconic <u>Little Tramp</u> character struggles to survive in the modern, industrialized world. The film is a comment on the desperate employment and fiscal conditions many people faced during the <u>Great Depression</u>, conditions created, in Chaplin's view, by the efficiencies of modern industrialization.

Chaplin biographer Jeffrey Vance wrote about the legacy of this classic comedy[5],

"Modern Times is perhaps more meaningful now than at any time since its first release. The twentieth-century theme of the film, farsighted for its time—the struggle to eschew alienation and preserve humanity in a modern, mechanized world—profoundly reflects issues facing the twenty-first century. The Tramp's travails in Modern Times and the comedic mayhem that ensues should provide strength and comfort to all who feel like helpless cogs in a world beyond control."

Today, fewer jobs depend solely on the operation of the types of machines used to such effect in The Industrial Revolution, but <u>three</u> fundamental concepts from Taylorism have survived and are ingrained in today's management philosophy, and in

[5]   Vance, Jeffery. *Chaplin: Genius of the Cinema.* (Harry N. Abrams, 2003)

the working of most modern companies:
- Processes
- Workflow
- Measurable Efficiency

This trio of concepts seems to <u>form</u> the bedrock of our modern understanding of organizations and they are therefore rarely questioned in modern business theory.

Modern Business Theory

Like Taylor before them, most <u>business</u> scientists and consultants have looked at organizations from two very distinct perspectives:

Top-down: This perspective is based on the belief that a business' financial success is drive by the structure of its organization, In order for <u>such</u> a business to function effectively (and generate income), it has to be properly organized, with all workers knowing their place, including a management team that oversees strategy and resource allocation. It needs a stated mission and vision, so everyone can tow the company line. The employees have to be controlled and organized into efficient structures within the company. An organization such as this rewards those who manage it well and who help make it possible for upper echelon management or even a single individual to steer the organization in a direction of his or her choosing.

The reason such an organization as this doesn't

change is obvious to even the casual student of human nature. The managers (or owners) at the top hold all the power and have no wish to change the status quo. Those workers at the bottom, most desirous of the change, haven't got the power to affect that change—except by overturning the whole apple cart. This is why anarchists followed closely on the heels of the Industrial Revolution and why unionism rose up when the smoke (quite literally) cleared.

Outside-in: In this perspective, a company is looked at as though all the pieces of the company (the workers, management <u>and</u> processes) were all one organism, interdependent on each other to function. The owner or management team will observe the company's workings, and basically deconstruct them, discerning strengths and weaknesses and making changes and adjustments to any or all departments or processes to help solve and problems and increase efficiency. Then that owner or management team will sit back and watch how those changes affect the inner workings of the company, reserving the right to continue tinkering –never necessarily declaring an end to the changes, but continuing in this flexible approach as the day-to-day workings of the company require fine-tuning.

This perspective has been the favorite of most of <u>the</u> big business theorists, from Peter Drucker, John P. Kotter and Henry Mintzberg to Peters and Waterman and Fredmund Malik and has been the go-to management theory of the last couple of decades.

Here are the components that make up today's <u>companies</u>:

- The Vision: What type of company does to organization want to be?
- The Mission: What is the purpose of the organization?
- Company Values: The type of culture and core values that members of the organization are expected to adhere to.
- Company Strategy: What are the company's long-term goals and how are they best to be achieved?
- Operations: How will the Company Strategy be implemented by use of structure, processes, and resources allocation?
- Company Objectives: What are the specific medium-term goals that are both measurable and achievable?
- Personal Goals: What are the objectives for individual members of the organization?
- Motivational System: What is in place to influence employee's behavior and actions to realize all of the above components?

In today's business environment, this framework is pretty ubiquitous. Which of the components takes priority may change company-to-company, but the various categories all find a place on the organizational chart of most modern business entities.

The organization calls the tune and the corporate lockstep is the favored dance. The creativity of the human spirit is not valued, in fact may be actively discouraged. Employees become anonymous numbers on a payroll sheet, kept in place when it suits the corporate "vision", easily replaceable when not. Success is measured only by the profit-and-loss statement. Human beings are discounted.

Such tunnel vision works against its stated goal in the end as energy, which could be spent innovating, inventing and expanding, must be spent on reorganization, endless adjustment to processes, and in motivating the employees to keep on churning out the work. This whipping-the-galley-slave mentality may keep the boat moving, but it won't contribute to any advancement in the transportation industry. It is time for such theories to join others on the trash bin of history. Those concepts no longer hold true for the Information Technology Age.

Think of a business, instead of being made up only of faceless entities submerging their individuality and unique talents for the "good" of the company, as a successful family. Each member of that family brings different viewpoints and opinions, based on their experience, prejudices and worldview. Each brings his or her unique personality, individual talents and both character assets and defects. Participation is encouraged, as the family recognizes such interaction promotes harmony within the group. Everyone is free to speak his or her mind and the member holding the minority opinion has as much right to be heard as the members holding the majority opinion. Each member has their job or jobs within the family and is expected to carry then out with integrity and diligence, demonstrating personal leadership. Problems are discussed openly and, should a decision go against what a member believes strongly, there is the right of appeal, before a final decision is made. Someone is given the right to take action on decisions, making effective leadership possible. Double-headed management is avoided, but the family, as a unit, strives to remain democratic in thought and action.

The framework within which our fictional family works differs in almost every particular from the artificial framework bolstering the modern corporation discussed above, created by powerful men to gain them control of organizations and keep everyone but that inner circle from having any say in how the organization is run.

That notion worked well for the pioneers (and eventual 'robber barons') of the Industrial Revolution, but it won't work well going forward. The generation, which grew up online, won't accept such strictures. There is a global world, cracked wide open by the Information Technology Revolution. All people are being given a seat at the table, *because there is no table*. The battlements have been stormed. The revolution has begun and corporate power players better lead, follow or get out of the way.

Bob Dylan, poet/prophet of the generation that bore the Online Generation, wrote of such a future:

Come gather 'round people

Wherever you roam

And admit that the waters

Around you have grown

And accept it that soon

You'll be drenched to the bone

If your time to you

Is worth saving

Then you better start swimming

Or you'll sink like a stone

For the times they are a-changing

The Online Generation

"Man is the lowest cost, 150-pound, non-linear, all-purpose computer system which can be mass produced by unskilled labor."

—NASA report advocating manned space flight, 1965

Let's revisit our caveman friend, Og, before we examine the Online Generation of today.

Og, despite being a pretty good cave painter, wasn't a great patron of the arts. He didn't spend his nights reading Keats or composing an opera, and he never turned a page of "War and Peace". His needs were immediate: Hunt food, kill food, eat food and try not to become food himself. Such tasks were surely important (true life-and-death decisions) but didn't require long, involved thought. Decisions were made on the move and the attention span required was a short one. Was food available? Get it. No food? Move on. Was there danger? Get out.

After the body's needs were met, Og's brain directed the digestion of the food and the nutrients to the body's systems. Next he found a safe place to rest and the cycle started again the next day. Og's brain wasn't required to do much beyond these basic tasks and so his brain did not get much bigger—it had no need to evolve.

When Og's descendants began to gather in settlements, stay put in one place and build rudimentary societies, their tasks became more complex (teamwork, for example, is a concept requiring some rumination) and humankind's brain evolved to take on the more advanced thinking such societal changes required.

One thing didn't change that much as mankind advanced— movement and brain activity worked best when they worked symbiotically. Modern studies show our brainpower is still improved by physical exercise, though our attention spans have gotten a lot longer since Og's time. We now can pay strict attention to subjects for 15-minute intervals. What we *can't* do is pay attention for the length of time required by our educational and corporate institutions.

From an early age, we stick kids at a classroom desk and have them sit still (and keep quiet) for 45-minute periods over a school day that can stretch for more than 8 hours, while being lectured by a teacher trying to hammer facts into their brains about which they have no interest. As the kids get older, we add the fact that almost all high-school students are incredibly sleep deprived, closing down the sensory cells in their brains even further. If you've ever seen the students in a first period college lecture hall, you'll see the situation gets no better once they reach the ivy-covered halls of our universities.

Once those kids make it out of the deadening educational environment, they become the young workers in our companies. Unless they have joined a manufacturing company and work the assembly line (another mind-numbing invention of the late Industrial Revolution, courtesy of Henry Ford and his Model T), they become "knowledge workers". We put them in a cubicle; sit them behind a computer screen for 8 hours or more, interrupted only by endless meetings that can last for hours. Lunch is often the most stimulating part of their day. We wonder why these workers are tired, stressed, lacking in enthusiasm for their jobs and contributing nothing in the way of creative ideas and solutions.

They have become the machines we have created them to be—the type of machines most valued in the workplaces of the past, the ones created during The Industrial Revolution. The originators of that revolution, the British pioneers, trained their administrative personnel to stray not at all from a certain definition of the proper employee: diligent, upright, unquestioning with no imagination required. Pip pip, stiff upper lip, for God and Empire. Stepping out of line was not rewarded.

But the workplace has changed since those days and (not a moment too soon). Creative thinking, imaginative problem solving and experimentation are now valued characteristics of a good employee (and hallmarks of a successful company). Instead of rooting these traits out of our employees, we now try to instill such traits in them. It's no easy task as we have done our lockstep mentality training well.

It's easy to see in a simple experiment:

Put a group of pre-school children in a room with a box of wooden blocks. Tell them to build a house and watch what happens. Even though the task is complex and there may be a squabble or two about who gets which block, all the kids will immediately turn their attention to the task, One child will start building walls; another one will try to put a tower on the house and a third will start moving more blocks to the work site. Inevitably the house will fall down and, undeterred, the kids will start to rebuild it again, usually sharing opinions about what should be done and why the other kid is a poopy head for doing it differently. But it doesn't matter, as work will continue on the house. Everybody is involved and engaged and the group's attention will be focused for a very long time.

Now, give the same type of age-appropriate complex task to a group of adult employees and watch what happens. First thing they will do is hold a meeting. At that meeting, the task will be deconstructed, responsibilities will be assigned and roles decided upon (Jim will the project leader. Tom will be site coordinator and Betty will be in charge of material procurement.) That first meeting will be a long one and then it will be over... but not, of course, until the next meeting is scheduled. Naturally everyone must check their schedules and calendars and a mutually agreeable time decided.

At the second meeting (no doubt rescheduled because one of the principals is either unable to attend or unable to complete their initial task and bring the required feedback to the meeting to update the other team members.) When the team finally gets back together, some members of the team have problems with the process to discuss, disagree with who is in charge of what or protest the weight of the responsibility they have been given. Perhaps a vote should be taken? How will that happen? Majority rules? Perhaps discussions and votes should be taken within subcommittees? They will discuss the formation of such subcommittees…no doubt, *ad nauseum*.

So far, much time has been wasted on meetings, discussions, arguments and the site hasn't even been cleared, much less one block moved into place. To say productivity has suffered would be an understatement.

The preschoolers, for all their "redesign" and "rebuilding" have achieved more and certainly have established a useful learning curve about what is actually going to be required to get the project done

It is said, "Out of the mouths of babes comes wisdom," and in this case, we surely could learn a thing or two from those much younger people. A 2012 study, conducted by the McKinsey Global Institute, a management consultancy firm, found that 28% of an office worker's time is spent on emails and that 61% of time is spent tracking down information or repetitive communication, with only 39% of time spent on role-specific tasks. What that means is, most workers spend the majority of their time trying to make themselves understood to their fellows, trying to get what they need to do their assigned task or covering their behinds, rather than actually getting any useful task done for the company.

This is a very important finding and changing a corporate culture where such is the norm is going to take some unlearning. The current powers that be will find the reeducation the most difficult—they, after all, have been doing things this way for their entire careers and are invested in keeping things pretty much the way they are. Fear of change is a fairly static human condition, but change they must.

The Online Generation is growing up fast and nipping at the heels of their elders. They won't stop till the last dog dies. The new technology has given this generation instant access to practically unlimited information and the tools to use it. Across corporations, across borders, these digital natives will change business environments by their unshakeable assumption that their way is the way things must be (their rock will meet their elders' hard place). The data proves them right.

In its study on social media, the McKinsey Global Institute estimates that knowledge workers can improve productivity by 20%–25% through use of social technologies, and this is only one tool in the Online Generation's new toolbox. Imagine when they use all the others to throw a wrench in the works of the ways things have always been done[6].

Gone will be the top-down management and

---

[6] Matson, Eric and Lawrence Prusak. *Boosting the productivity of knowledge workers*. (September 2010) Retrieved June 3, 2015, from McKinsey Quarterly: http://www.mckinsey.com/insights/organiza-tion/boosting_the_productivity_of_knowledge_workers

inside-out models, giving way to a bottom up one, allowing for the greatest machine of all to hold sway—the human brain.

Methodologies to which we have been shacked too long will go by the wayside. We will bid farewell to business theories built on the dusty old concepts of process, workflow and measurable efficiency and say hello to the humancentric organization and the dazzling lights of a new generation who, being encouraged to perform their personal best according to their own unique talents, will illuminate the dim halls of corporations and light up the world.

CHAPTER FOUR

SELF-ORGANIZING ENVIRONMENTS: LEARNINGFROMNATURE, TECHNOLOGY, AND US

"There seems to be some perverse human characteristic that likes to make easy things difficult."

—Warren Buffett (born 1930), investor

Keeping it simple sometimes seems beyond us as human beings.

Maybe it is a deep-rooted disbelief that anything too easily won can be truly valuable. Maybe we just want to look smarter and do so by creating more complexity in our tasks so we appear superhuman when we complete them. Maybe we are just afraid to go it alone and add to our burdens just so we have to ask for help (and therefore also share any blame for screw-ups with our collaborators.) Or perhaps we don't know how to strip things to their essence, clarify what needs doing and focus only on that one task.

We seem to be born to muddy the waters and spend much of our energy trying to see more clearly, by piling facts upon facts until we are hoisted on our own petard—a leaning tower of knowledge certain to fall of its own weight.

We could learn a thing or two from our smaller brethren—the ants. Just as we saw from the preschoolers involved in our building experiment, the ants also have lessons to teach us about basic engagement, a concept very important for our humancentric organization.

Welcome to the Ant Hill

I have always intrigued by the functioning of an ant colony. These little creatures have to build a home, keep it clean, gather food, bring up the kids and defend the colony and, though there may be thousands of individual ants, they have to do so together, as one fully functioning organization

I have never seen them sitting around a conference table holding meetings, reading manuals to better understand the processes, or spending hours on the phone or sending emails to communicate. Nevertheless, the colony seems to function perfectly well without spending all their time on the tasks that modern businesses can't seem to do without. We two-legged folks invest an inordinate amount of our working time just getting our work organized—61% of our time, according to those studies cited previously. Ants, however, know just what is expected of every worker and get right down to the task at hand—with no time wasted.

Deborah Gordon, a biologist at Stanford University and a specialist in ant colonies, has studied ants for decades. In her studies on harvester ants, which build colonies of more than 10,000 ants, she identified four main tasks for the worker ants that are stationed both at the exit and outside the colony:

- Midden Work
- Nest Maintenance
- Patrolling
- Foraging

About a quarter of the colony's ants are engaged in such tasks. Another quarter are working deep within the colony and the remaining ants are resting up for their "shift".

After observing this well established division of labor, Gordon wanted to see what would happen if the circumstances the ants faced were changed. How would the colony adapt to the new circumstances? How would their organization change?

Gordon performed several experiments where she introduced extra food, increased dirt infiltration of the nest and created various disturbances to which the ants needed to react. No matter what irregular factor Gordon introduced, the ants rose to the occasion. They adopted all-hands on deck attitude. Several more ants would abandon their original job postings and join in the new task at hand, especially if the disturbances held a threat to the colony itself. Depending on how important to the colony's survival the new happenstance was, the colony reacted differently. If extra food became available, all outside ants would report for duty and help gather and store the extra provisions. If, however, the job presented was just getting rid of extra dirt, none of the outside ants would join the beefed-up cleanup crew, but more ants from the inside would join in.

So how did the ants know what to do and what not to do?

It seems that ants emit a different smell depending on the task they are performing. When one ant meets another one from the same colony, it will smell the other ant, using its antenna. Depending on how many times an ant encounters another with a specific task smell, determines where the worker ant decides she should go lend a hand. It is not the interaction between herself and a single other ant that triggers the decision; it is the pattern of interactions. If the ant runs into a greater number of foraging ants at any given time, she understands that there is a need for more foragers and so she becomes one. She is, in fact, acting for the greater good of the organization.

This elegant process allows even creatures with simple brains and limited problem-solving skills to build complex systems and adapt to changes.

Welcome to Kindergarten

"Every child is an artist. The problem is how to remain an artist once we grow up."

—Pablo Picasso (1881–1973), Spanish artist.

Harkening back again to the simplicity (some say the simple genius) of childhood, let's visit kindergarten. A wise teacher largely leaves her students alone at playtime to teach them how to deal with their fellows; lessons that prepare them for the real-life situations they will encounter in their adult lives. Were you standing on the edge of the playground, the first thing you would notice is that children left alone to play together will naturally self-organize, no adult needed to enforce who does what to whom.

Kids will scan the area to see the toys or game in which they are most interested, then they will watch other kids playing with those toys or involved in that game. After mentally summing up the interactions between the kids and checking the possibilities for grabbing his or her own portion of the fun, the kindergartener will then join the game of tag or belly-up to the train table to try to get his or her hand on that freight car or caboose.

Each time, the game will evolve with intuitive rules and a complex set of interactions and yet will end up with very clear organization, every child knowing what they must do and when to keep the game going. What is the secret these little ones have that we seem to lose as we grow and become more sophisticated and, ostensibly, better able to solve problems?

Obviously it is not a question of structure, processes, and instructions being clearly identified, laid out and adhered to; there is no corporate framework or management handbook to advise these kids how to do their task better or more efficiently. Theirs is a matter of observation and interaction. The children come equipped with an ingrained behavior, like the tendency to mimic others, like those ants that learn from their fellows to smell what to do next. The children watch to see if they can understand what is going on in the game and then follow what the others kids are doing. By making use of those two behaviors-observation and interaction-as foundation stones, complex systems can be built. Despite being different species, the behavior of groups of ants and small children is based on the same organizing principles and such organizing principles can be used to make any organization a better one.

As children grow, these principles can be applied to ever more complex situations and, combined with the capability of sophisticated communication many more things become possible. Nevertheless, the underlying concept remains the same, and we will see in later chapters how these organizing principles can be used to our advantage in combination with modern technology to unlock the full potential of the computer age.

The Power of Networks

"We have taken apart the universe and have no idea how to put it back together. After spending trillions of research dollars to disassemble nature in the last century, we are just now acknowledging that we have no clue how to continue—except to take it apart further."

—Albert-László Barabási, Professor of Physics at Notre Dame University in his book *Linked*, 2003

How that ant colony or group of small children at play work together can be explained through the network theory. This theory is relatively new and is still a scientific concept in the making, but at its most basic, the theory is that all human beings interact with each other through networks.

This was explained when Mark Granovetter published his seminal paper, *The Strengths of Weak Ties*[7]. This paper, for the first time, helped to explain how social networks form and connect to each other. With this step, network theory moved from a theoretical scientific concept to a practical concept. The base idea is simple. Every

---

[7]   Mark S. Granovetter. *American Journal of Sociology*, Volume 78, Issue 6 (May, 1973), 1360-1380.

node (human) is part of a *cluster* (group). Within a group, everybody knows everybody, what he called a *complete cluster*. Those clusters are then connected to other clusters through *weak ties*.

Weak ties are connections of people who belong to different groups and might have only limited interests in common. Those weak ties are fundamental to the functioning of social networks. They connect a relatively homogeneous group (complete cluster) to the outside world where new ideas and information will reach the cluster. This weak link theory has been capitalized upon fantastically by LinkedIn where you may know people designated as "1st connections" and not have any idea who that guy claiming to be your "3rd connection is, but as long as he knows Bob, who works in the next cubicle over from you, he and you share an interest—limited though your interest in Bob may be.

Almost 30 years after, Granovetter's paper was published, the concept of *hub*s or *connectors* was introduced. The base idea was that while regular nodes (with a little variation) will all have a similar quantity of links some of those nodes will have a much larger number of links, which are called connectors or hubs. These hubs bring whole groups together, connecting more and more groups together until, eventually, everyone will be connected. It is the "six degrees of separation" theory on steroids. (We may in fact, as is often posited on the internet, discover we really *are* all related to the actor Kevin Bacon!)

Everybody belongs to a group of people, and within that group, all its members are highly connected. Those groups however are only connected to one another with weak links. Most people have about a similar amount of connections (people they actively know), whereas very few have a much larger number of connections. Those that do are the connectors or hubs. Those connectors play a fundamental role in our social structures.

As Malcolm Gladwell points out in his book, *The Tipping Point*[8], connectors are the people who are responsible for breakthroughs of ideas and concepts, since they are the elements keeping together the whole of society. At the turn of the century, Barabási added the *preferential attachment* concept to the formation of networks. He pointed out that well-connected nodes would always add more connections than less well-connected nodes, so people who know a lot of people (connectors) meet more new people than those who know only an average amount of people.

This explains how hubs are built into networks and how connectors form. Which node will develop into a hub depends on the node's fitness, its ability to attract other nodes to link to it. The fitter the node, the more links will be generated to it.

Behind any real network, there is no guiding force organizing it, but instead it is, like those kin-

---

[8]   Gladwell, Malcolm (2002). *The Tipping Point: How Little Things Can Make a Big Difference*. New York: Back Bay Books.

dergartners, self-organized. This does not mean that the network is random; quite to the contrary, complex networks are built in modular fashion, where hubs are the communication nodes between the different modules.

Network theory gives us the basis to understand complex systems, like cells, societies, or organizations. The focus is not on the single part (any one person, one company or one ant for that matter), but on the very few simple rules of interactions. The research into complex systems has been driven from biology and the need to understand living organisms, but has lately moved into other areas of interest, like management theory as well.

While business theory and literature can analyze companies (how they are built up, what they believe in, their decision and strategy processes, their tasks and how they are best divided, and what kinds of underlying tools should be used by them), the idea that a company is like a living system, made up of nodes (which can be people and machines) that interact through simple rules, would fundamentally change the way we look at companies. A network, as opposed to a hierarchical structure, is much more adaptable to any kind of influence (and stable enough to absorb such influences.) This can be seen in stable communication networks as opposed to traditional information technology models that used structured approaches. This underscores how superior to this model is to any other organizing principle.

Network theory is one important ingredient in the formation of a successful humancentric complex system. Other ingredients that we will look at more deeply later in this book include self-organization, technology individual effort within the group, shared guiding principles, the importance of a common goal and the fact that a new generation of people will be the workers in these organizations to be—all of which play vital roles in the changing future of work.

Human Systems Today

"Be the change that you wish to see in the world."

—Mahatma Gandhi, Indian lawyer and independence activist, 1869–1948

Back to our kindergartners, who are, in fact, a network. We may define every child as a node and their interaction while they play with other kids as links, meaning our group of children will form a cluster. The hub in this scenario would be the teacher.

At play, children will self-organize by building links (through observation, imitation and communication) to fulfill a task—whether that is to organize a ball game or erect a house of blocks. These networks form *ad hoc* systems to fulfill certain tasks (play), and they will disintegrate again once the task is fulfilled or another task has become more interesting to them. At any time, links can be built or removed, creating in the network a dynamic state of constant change.

This is how human organizational systems work today.

The British educational system (upon which ours is based) was built to manage an empire with tendrils scattered across a globe from one central location—the heart of that empire in London. Such a far-flung empire run from one place required adherence to strict rules and regulations. Workers needed to toe the line. Creative self-expression was not an asset, nor was any deviation from the established order. To keep such a system running, students, the future workers of the Empire, were taught uniform facts in a uniform way to be ready to fit uniform job in a uniform organization. "For God and Empire," was the catchphrase and such a system worked for a time.

Only certain men, those seen in daguerreotypes sporting magnificent moustaches, known as the Captains of Industry were to chart the course and set the rules and they expected to be obeyed.

In more modern times, titans like Jack Welch of GE basically ran his own show. He knew everything that was happening in "his" company and signed off on every decision. If you weren't Jack Welch, you didn't have the last word.

This was the very essence of top-down management and, while it afforded Jack Welch the iron control upon which he insisted, such a system certainly hindered innovation.

But it was a system we all knew well. It had worked for our fathers and our fathers before that and we really aren't overly fond of messing with success and making changes when it isn't absolutely necessary.

Since we are humans (and employ the can't-keep-it-simple philosophy all too often), we create manmade systems, like clubs, corporations and governments, that are almost always built around this top-down model. Since that model comes equipped with inherent problems, as we've seen, organizations built around it often need a complete reorganization to remain successful. But such complete transformational changes won't happen all at once, of course. People are often resistant to abrupt change and things may need to be implemented slowly to ease people into such transition. In some case, change may, in fact, be minimal.

In 100 years, we will still have traditional companies will still use a traditional organization and will still be successful, and, in others, creating change will be, as the saying goes, like pulling teeth.

Take, for example, the United States Postal Service. Creaky and barely functional as it is, the post office may still contain to function much like it does today because it is a legacy business and legacy business are notoriously intransigent. Couple that with the fact that the post office is awash in regulations and built-in protections and changing anything about the service will be difficult.

Legacy jobs are threaded throughout many industries, the more legacy systems. The military, for example, won't be the first to be overhauled or network for the new paradigm. From the Joint Chiefs on down to generals and chiefs and captains of all branches, commanders will shout down the suggestion that their organizations are anything but highly effective. Regulation wrapped in regulation protects the healthcare industry from change and we've all seen how the insurance agency has gone down swinging in a fight to protect itself from the changes brought by Obamacare.

The higher the hurdle, the less *evolutionary* and the more *revolutionary* change must be.

So what if that reorganization used as its framework the network idea? First, some of the terminology used in the corporate world would have to change. Here are the network translations of some common terms:

Nodes: Employees, machines, suppliers, and customers, stakeholders

Links: Relationships and transactions.

Clusters: Teams, families, workgroups, friends, social clubs, and parties.

Hubs: Top management, government leaders, trendsetters, public figures, thought leaders.

Let's use an example of a single employee, working in the internal sales department of a company. This single node (the salesperson) will be part of a cluster (the other internal salespeople) that has multiple links both within the cluster and outside of the cluster to other clusters (like external sales, marketing, purchasing, manufacturing, and finance). Beyond that, the cluster also has links to marketing agencies, customers, and vendors outside the company organization.

We can now assume that within his/her department, every employee is connected to everybody else (see Figure 4) to form a complete cluster. Every employee of that cluster is connected to other clusters through work and private relationships.

In Figure 5, only our original employee's links to other clusters have been drawn. Through those few links, the whole organization is connected, and every employee is, at the most, two degrees from every other employee. (In larger organizations, obviously, there will be more than two degrees between every employee). By adding the external world outside of the organization to the graph (see Figure 6), with only a few links, whole new systems and clusters are added to the network.

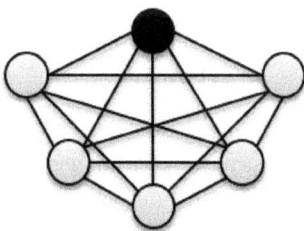

Figure 4: Internal sales employee within his internal sales cluster.

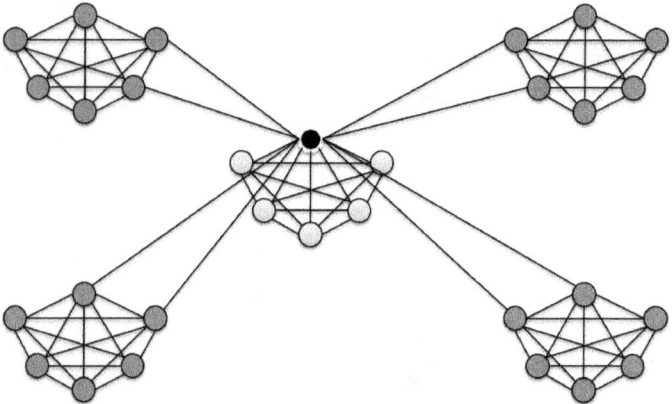

Figure 5: Internal sales employee within the company organization with links to other clusters (departments).

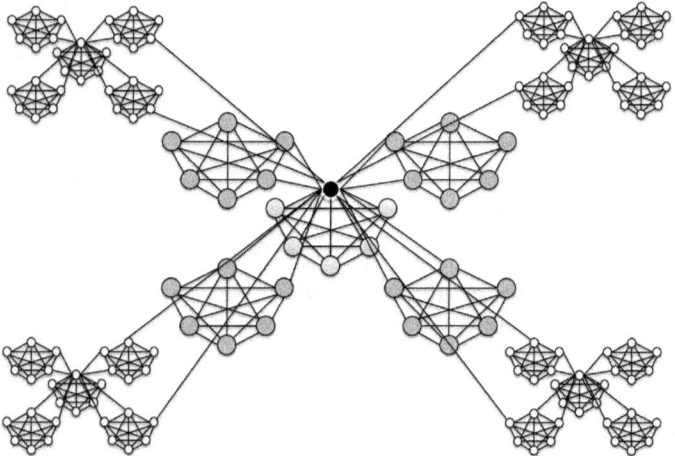

Figure 6: Internal Sales employee with internal and external links.

In the real world, these clusters and links do not happen randomly or by self-organization, but through top-down organizational structures and processes. Organizations spend a lot of energy to keep these networks efficient and functioning at all times, as well as to be able to constantly adapt to changes in the network (change of nodes and links) and to changes in the environment. Tools like hierarchy, organizational structure, job descriptions, process redesign, appraisal, internal communication, and meetings often have, as a primary purpose, improving the functioning of the network. But networks only truly work in self-organizing environments and most companies today are anything but self-organizing. If they were, as we saw in the McKinsey study, 61% of a knowledge worker's time could be allocated much more efficiently.

The combination of information technology and computers, together with network theory and complex systems, allow us to have the capability today to build such self-organizing systems, eliminating that wasted time, making systems not only more efficient, but more adaptable and therefore more effective.

If even very primitive creatures like ants can build complex colonies, humans surely can use those self-organizing principles we knew in childhood and harness them before they are siphoned off by our current educational system.

By changing how we are educating people and creating work environments that encourage creativity and innovation over monotony and repetition, we will begin a process that will start moving the needle towards a new paradigm of work.

When we combine these changes with information technology and apply ideas adapted from network theory, we will align ourselves with forces that can take the best of human endeavor put forth thus far and make it even better.

As Brynjolfsson and McAffe conclude in their book, *Race Against the Machine*, moving into the second half of the chessboard, it is the race *with* the machines that will be the essence of the third industrial revolution.

By combining forces between man and machines, we will be able to say, as the robot HAL in *2001: A Space Odyssey* so eloquently stated, "I am putting myself to the fullest possible use, which is all, I think, that any conscious entity can ever hope to do."

CHAPTER FIVE

THEMARKETFORWORKIS BROKEN

"Can you imagine what I would do if I could do all I can?"

—Sun Tzu

As with all technological revolutions, the transition to a new humancentric organization will be slow, and resistance to the changes it engenders high. Some areas of human value creation will be able to resist longer, thanks to regulatory and weak market forces. Others will have to adapt, and new ventures will eventually overtake the stick-in-the-muds.

As we have seen, the way organizations will work in the future is different than the way we have worked in the past.

First of all, corporations must change. Companies currently are too structured and very inflexible. Most companies don't have the right talent available at the right time to correctly pursue the opportunities that would most benefit them. This is not always a lack of personnel per se. The company may have plenty of people but many, if not most, of those people are not putting their talents to the best use or their native talent may in fact remain undiscovered. They were hired for one job—perhaps long ago—and never got a chance to develop other skills or talents during their time at the company. Instead they were assigned a job (and a cubicle); given a company manual; told to absorb and structure their work around a complex (and perhaps archaic) set of regulations; ordered to attend meeting after mind-numbing meeting (during which not much is created and lots of time is wasted); and, eventually, the employee loses any creative spark that once shone within them and they become the classic company drone. New ideas and talents go undiscovered, innovation dies before it is born and everyone learns to live with a certain level of mediocrity that they call "good enough."

From a prospective workers point of view, things are no better. Someone with the skills, talent and even necessary experience may learn of a job for which they would be perfectly suited only to submit a resume that is buried in a pile of thousands, never to be reviewed by a company's HR department because the robot scanning the resumes discards it since its keywords don't exactly match the job description. The resume is never even read by human eyes. Conversely, a mediocre talent or one lacking the skills to be a success at the job has figured out the keyword game and matches his or her cover letter exactly to the job description, whether or not they have the relevant experience. Such a dissembler actually stands a better chance of being interviewed for the position. But, even if an interview is granted, it is probably only one of many as the job applicant is passed around like a box of Cracker Jacks, meeting everyone who might ever work with him or her (called "stakeholders") and all must weigh in and agree before the applicant gets advanced up the ladder to department heads, vice presidents and sometimes even the CEO. By this time, weeks or even months have passed and often the qualified candidate gets hired by another company with whom they started the process months before the current one.

Or a qualified applicant is suddenly informed that they are out of the game, but never told why. Did their references not check out? Was there a discrepancy in their resume they were unaware of or perhaps the job was filled? The whole hiring process is anything but transparent and certainly not empowering. Applicants are left to the mercy of robot screeners, faceless HR staffers and never have a chance to be recommended by someone who knows them for the job unless, as the old adage goes, they've "got an uncle in the business."

Problematic also in this "old way" of doing business is that our employment process is too long and our contracts are inflexible.

Take a look at the hiring timeline itself in today's business model. It takes an average of nine months from the decision to hire someone until the day the person actually starts. Depending on the industry, nine months in the life of a company can be a very long time. Many vital things might have changed within the company by the time the new person starts the job.

From an employee's perspective, what happened is that the employee got motivated and hired for a specific job, but, by time he or she was trained and started to work, environments may have changed. So over time, people remained in their job, and chased the paycheck, but their talents weren't put to best use.

For its part, the company doing the hiring under this old model believes that taking endless time to research, gather information about and do background checks on candidates to be a good decision. They may also be hindered by excessive regulation, all of which leads to them wanting to keep whomever they hire as an employee for a very long time (to avoid having to go through the laborious process again). They become careful almost to the point of stasis. By being so meticulous and cautious in their hiring practices, the Powers That Be, by filtering the responsibility and decision making process among so many individuals in the company, are actually doing the company a disservice. Such thinking usually trickles down in other areas, encouraging employees to be hesitant to make decisions, creates an atmosphere of redundancy and butt-covering that smothers innovation, and general behaves in ways that show they believe the company prefers such fossilization. The company's management team is therefore part of the problem in this old organizational model.

The Broken Work Market

All of this leads to the inevitable conclusion that the market for work is broken, irretrievably and forever, unless we bow to certain facts and take certain steps—revolutionary steps to create an entirely new market for work. If that strikes you as an overly dramatic statement, let's look at what experts say about this endemic problem. Statistics show quite clearly that the market isn't functioning properly—that the broken work market is a fact, not just a perception.

Looking first at the workers themselves, we find that most Americans are unhappy at work. This was not always the case. That number has slid over time. Nearly three decades ago, 61.1% of workers said they liked their jobs. So what changed? Apparently, nearly everything that has to do with earning one's daily bread. A survey, conducted by the Conference Board, a New York-based nonprofit research group, asked workers how they felt about various parts of their working experience, including job security, wages, promotion policy, vacation policy, sick leave, health plans and re-tirement plans. On all of those measures, workers were happier in 1987 than they are now. Such un-happy workers take more sick days and work less efficiently when they are on the job. They also feel less loyalty to a company, jump ship for what they perceive to be a better opportunity without look-ing back (costing American corporations millions in recruitment and replacement costs) and leave companies critically shorthanded, lacking workers with specific knowledge and skill sets to complete current projects or to be available for future inno-vations[9].

Such disgruntled workers are defined as "not engaged" or "actively disengaged" by a State of the Global Workplace report conducted by Gallup that reported on such engagement, or lack thereof, in 140 countries. The report used the following definitions:

- Engaged employees work with passion and feel a profound connection to their com-pany. They drive innovation and move the organization forward.
- Not Engaged employees are essential-ly "checked out." They're sleepwalking through their workday, putting time—but not energy or passion—into their work.

9   Adams, Susan. *Most Americans Are Unhappy At Work*. Retrieved February 8, 2016, from Forbes.com: http://www.forbes.com/sites/susanadams/2014/06/20/most-americans-are-unhappy-at-work/

- Actively disengaged employees aren't just unhappy at work; they're busy acting out their unhappiness. Every day, these workers undermine what their engaged co-workers accomplish.

The report found that 87 percent of workers worldwide and 70 percent of employees in the U.S. (as well as 84 percent in Canada, 83 percent in the U.K.) are either *not engaged* (as in turning in mediocre work or posting to their Facebook accounts during work hours) or *actively disengaged* (printing out client contact lists for use in their own consulting company they are setting up or dropping the ball on the part of the project that was their responsibility to handle, or missing deadlines and effectively scuttling projects.) What these numbers mean is that only 30 percent of U.S. workers are driving their organizations forward. Such malaise doesn't come cheap.

The State of the Global Workplace report found that actively *disengaged* employees cost the U.S. $450 billion to $550 billion per year and that number doesn't even take into account the "not engaged" employees. And such a financial hemorrhage is only one symptom of a broken marketplace. What is harder to measure is what the "energy drain", caused by unhappy workers pulling the company down and the" opportunity cost" where the potential for having happy workers isn't being harvested. Both of these are costing companies as well. Imagine what progress could be made if the majority of workers were actively *engaged*, enthusiastically contributing their ideas and talents to a company's projects and all rowing the boat in the same direction. Freed of the deadweight of unhappy, *disengaged* employees, a company could soar, free to imagine, envision and innovate. Without such shackles binding companies to outmoded ways to work (and treat their workers), companies would have vital R&D departments, manufacture products we have yet to imagine and fulfill the dreams of satisfying jobs for workers the world over—jobs for which they are well suited by education and avocation. [10]

Correcting this part of the broken market saves both time and money. *According to the research report, Talent Acquisition Factbook 2015: Benchmarks and Trends in Spending, Staffing, and Key Recruiting Metrics* cited by Dr. Robin Erickson on Deloitte's Bersin Blog[11], finding (and snagging) the right candidate for open positions is increasingly difficult for corporations.

In 2014, U.S. companies increased their average talent acquisition costs 7% from 2013, driven in part by an increase to nearly $4,000 cost per hire

[10] Ayu, Ariana. *The Enormous Cost of Unhappy Employees.* August 27, 2014. Retrieved February 8, 2016, from Inc.com: http://www.inc.com/ariana-ayu/the-enormous-cost-of-unhappy-employees.html

[11] Erickson, Robin. *Benchmarking Talent Acquisition: Increasing Spend, Cost Per Hire, and Time to Fill.* April 23, 2015. Retrieved February 8, 2016 from Bersin by Deloitte: http://www.bersin.com/blog/post/Benchmarking-Talent-Acquisition-Increasing-Spend2c-Cost-Per-Hire2c-and-Time-to-Fill.aspx

in 2014. Companies are finding it takes 52 days on average to fill open positions—up from 48 days in 2011.

Taking into account that the "right" candidate may in fact turn out to be one of those *not engaged* or worse, *actively disengaged* and this part of the problem becomes clear, but it is only part of the problem of employee acquisition. The other is the amount of money a company spends to get a candidate to join the team.

A report[12], published by the Centre for Economics and Business Research (CEBR) and the UK's Federation of Small Business, points out the true cost of hiring an employee far exceeds his or her salary. On average, the index calculates, a business with one employee and one owner faces an average employment cost of £35,500 ($56,770) per worker, far more than the average non-managerial employee makes for their job[13].

A company will spend capital and, as time is money, valuable time to recruit an employee who has a very good chance of becoming, not only a parasite on the corporate body (along for the ride, sucking vital energy out, but giving nothing back)

---

[12] *Cost of Small Business Employment*. (2014, October 30). Retrieved Julay 15, 2015 from the Centre for Economics and Business Research: http://www.cebr.com/reports/cost-of-small-business-employment/

[13] Hesse, Jason. *The True Cost of Hiring an Employee?* October 30, 2014. Retrieved July 15, 2015 from Forbes.com: http://www.forbes.com/sites/jasonhesse/2014/10/30/here-is-the-true-cost-of-hiring-an-employee/

or worse, an active enemy (a modern Trojan horse bringing down the system from within.)

One needn't be a prophet to see the market is broken and to call out for a better one. You need only to open your eyes and your mind to new thinking and ways of doing business—that are not just outside the box, but which throw the box away entirely.

Potential for a Perfect Market for Work

First we need to retool our thinking about how companies are supposed to work and how value will be created in the future.

Imagine if everyone in the work force were able to dedicate his or her time putting h/her best talents to use, being released from those obligatory and endless meetings, foregoing those tasks that made no use of these talents and freed from the commute, the time clock and the cubicle. Recall that in a previous chapter, we learned that employees invest an inordinate amount of their time—61% in fact— just getting their work organized. Now we have added that statistic about workers that aren't engaged or are actively disengaged. Imagine the quantum leap in productivity gains that could be achieved when all workers are not only are suited to their jobs, but *want* to be there, and are organized, prepared and enthusiastic about devoting their time to fruitful tasks in service to the company.

Now, in this perfect work world we are

discussing, envision if every single person got the education, resources and support to discover, make best use of and even enhance their talents. Everyone who wanted to work would have a job, perfectly suited to his or her talents and expertise, allowing for innovative thinking to flourish.

Companies would be able to put aside constant worries about having the right workers to fit ever-changing projects and market conditions, and, with the ability to choose from a global marketplace, would always having just the right people for the job at hand. Recruiting and all company overhead would be reduced and flexibility gained.

From a worker's perspective, the quality of life gains would be enormous. He or she could work whatever hours they choose, allowing time to share childcare, never miss a soccer game or spend time caring for an elderly parent. Since the worker chooses his or her hours, balancing work/ life priorities becomes easier and stress becomes less (which would yield health benefits as well.) Because of technological breakthroughs like Skype and conference calls, geographical boundaries that once limited work, dissolve and many jobs can be done from wherever the worker is located—reducing or eliminating commutes, helping save the environment and lessening the strain on infrastructure at the same time. Workers may pick the projects they wish to work upon, choosing only those about which they feel passionate or help them realize their potential. With the ability to change jobs easily, moving from project-to-project, the worker escapes stifling hierarchies and puts their talents to work only in a goal-oriented environment, meeting new colleagues along the way, all of whom end up comprising one's own custom professional network. Such a network (and their positive recommendations) help secure the worker's next project, doing away with the impersonal, often robotic, human resources process that cost so much, takes so long and which saddles companies with so many disappointing employees.

From a company perspective, a properly functioning new market for work yields them the ability to react instantly to changing requirements and market conditions—to make the notion of "guerilla marketing" a reality, knowing that the company will always have people with the skills, experience and talent to meet any changing needs, immediately and consistently. There would be no lag time while searching for the right person to do the job—the right person would always be at a company's fingertips. This would not only perfect a company's resource allocation, matching opportunities with resources just as the opportunities present themselves, but also allow an organization to size itself correctly. With talent brought on board only as needed, fundamental recruiting costs would shrink, as would company overhead, and a corporation wouldn't be spending money on underused, incorrectly placed or idle employees.

New ideas could be tested for a fraction of the cost and productivity would naturally increase. Even more exciting is the idea, further discussed below, that a company can source its workers from what was till now virtually inaccessible—a global talent pool. The world is now literally open for business.

Three key factors have evolved over the last few years that allow for the creation of the perfect market for work. This powerful trio has not existed in the history of the world until now, but the introduction of Technology, Communication and the Culture of the Sharing Economy make the perfect market possible at last.

We have finally reached the second half of the chessboard we discussed earlier. By making use of technology, communicating amongst ourselves in ways never before possible and sharing the knowledge we acquire, the brave new world of work is no longer just a utopian idea or far-off pipe dream. The future is now.

We are increasingly interconnected

Michael Jackson's song, "We Are the World" has become a home truth. Nearly half of the entire population of the world is using the internet today (up from just 16% nine years ago.) As should come as no surprise, 78% of the developed world is connected via the internet, but it is not just rich economies talking to each other anymore. 32% of the developing world has gone online and those numbers are climbing each day[14].

Stop and let those numbers sink in a moment and you will begin to see just how enormous the market is now and will be in the future.

In 1995, less than 1% of the world population used the internet. The number of internet users has increased tenfold from 1999 to 2013. The **first billion** was reached in 2005. The **second billion** in 2010. The **third billion** in 2014.

Twenty years ago, many of these new internet users—these same people, in the same spot on the globe — didn't even have easy access to a book. Such access was harder and more expensive than the global technology available to them today. Now those same people have access, via technology, to the same knowledge base as you or I[15].

The World Bank, in their report, *Maximizing Mobile*, reports that close to three-quarters of the world's population, including much of the developing world, now has access to a mobile phone, making the devices even more widespread than internet penetration. Up to 80 percent of households in countries like Azerbaijan, Belarus, Georgia, and Kazakhstan currently have mobile phones. That number rises to 90 percent in Russia and 94 per-

---

[14] Global Internet usage. (2015, November 23). In *Wikipedia, The Free Encyclopedia*. Retrieved 02:50, February 9, 2016, from https://en.wikipedia.org/w/index.php?title=Global_Internet_usage&oldid=692106543

[15] Internet Live Stats. http://www.internetlivestats.com/internet-users/

cent in Iraq[16].

Many of these people, hundreds of millions of them, may not even have reliable electricity in their homes, but they do have a cell phone. People whose income may only be a couple of dollars a day now have internet access. This changes the scenario for everyone—most especially for people who may not be as privileged as you or I.

Such technology is basically free—free to all—making all the information available from use of such technology free too. Such technology and the access it makes available to the banker in Switzerland and the farmer in Borneo is a game changer—a truly revolutionary tool—the great equalizer.

The Jamaican fisherman may now make use of sophisticated technology by which he can have exact market prices, both for sale in his village and further afield. He can use this information to choose the correct time to fish and even the best type of fish to hunt at any given time. Based on this data, the fisherman may choose to stay in the harbor on a certain day or change the type of fish he is seeking on another, depending on market conditions. Expand this example to cover all the other fisherman in the village, too, so that all of them have the correct information. They also will fish based only on current market conditions. Once all fisherman

---

[16] *Report Says 75 Percent of World's Population Have Mobile Phones.* (2012, July 12) Retrieved August 1, 2015 from Radio Free Europe/ Radio Liberty: http://www.rferl.org/content/report-says-75-per-cent-of-worlds-population-have-mobile-phones/24648234.html

are doing do, you have approximated a "perfect market for work." Our original fisherman can arrange distribution and shipment, contact and keep customers, and join the globally economy. Or he may just decide to contact wholesalers on his island, as he is no longer tethered only to the area around his home. Or he may decide to let his son, who is connected via the internet to a virtual programming position for a corporation in New York, do all the work and make three times the money the fisherman would ever make, while the father puts his feet up and retires.

All such scenarios, and hundreds more, are now available to almost everyone, with more people all over the planet joining the rosters of the interconnected every day. Workers are no longer limited by geography or access to education or any of the other factors that separated the "us" from the "them". A person can go as far with his career as his energy, determination and native talents can take him. There are no limits to how high he may rise.

Such a fundamental change in technology will shake the foundations of work itself and must soon be understood and embraced by the hierarchical companies of the world—as they must adapt or get out of the way. But one feature of this new market for work will come as no surprise to the younger workers of today and certainly of tomorrow: the total change in culture. Technology not only changes the way knowledge and work can be performed but also the foundations of our social interaction. This cultural change, already redrawing the lines on our maps of commerce, remakes the entire constellation of work as surely as if the stars had shifted in the sky—it is the culture of trust.

When I was coming up, my social and professional connections were largely geographically based. I gathered my friends and professional contacts from my neighborhood, the sports clubs to which I belonged and my schools and university. If I couldn't physically get to a place to shake a hand or slap a back, I couldn't connect. Even phone conversations usually ended in an invitation to meet for coffee. "Meeting" — and that meant in person—was the expected thing. When I was in university, the internet phenomenon began to grow, but even then we asked each other for f2f meetings (face-to-face), a stipulation fast going the way of the dodo.

The generations that came immediately after me, the Gen Xers and Millennials never knew any other way to connect with each other than they do now. Geographical limits went away and they "met" each other online, building friendships and business relationships with people that had never met and very possibly never would meet. They had to learn to trust and do business with people whose hand they would never shake and whose voice they might never hear and that was an earth-shattering fundamental change in the way things were done.

The easiest way to track such change is to examine just how much time each generation is spending online.

In 2014, Gen Xers spent 47.6% of their time online, Baby Boomers 39.5%, and Seniors, 26% of their time using the internet. Those numbers are growing, of course, but even in the past year, we see that the younger people—the workers of today and tomorrow—already spend half their time in a virtual world, as opposed to sitting in meetings, catching a plane for a client meeting or even networking at a tradeshow or corporate-sponsored happy hour. When they recreate, they do so by watching streaming videos or binge watching downloaded TV, listening to Pandora or online radio, buying music on iTunes to amp up their Spotify list, read an eBook, follow a blogger or repost photos or articles they found on FARK. In neither instance, work nor recreation, are the younger generations untethered long from their cyber umbilical cords.[17]

Throw in time to eat, sleep and exercise, and the picture becomes clearer. Gen X and the Millennials have a deep connection to a culture unlike any the world has ever seen.

That culture is not limited to the USA or the West either.

---

[17] *Weekly time spent online by U.S. affluents from 2011 to 2014, by generation (in hours).* (November 2014). Retrieved August 15, 2015 from Statista.com: http://www.statista.com/statistics/313193/us-affluents-generations-weekly-time-online/

Growth in data alone paints the picture—In 2012, the world generated and replicated about 2.8 zettabytes (ZB) of data. The "digital universe" is forecast to reach 40 ZB by 2020, (40 ZB is equal to 57 times the amount of all the grains of sand on all the beaches on earth. 40 ZB will represent 5,247 GB of data per person worldwide.) That number is up from previous estimates of just 5 ZB. According to the International Development Council (IDC), the data volume will have grown 50-fold in 2020 from 2010 levels. By 2020, the data created in emerging markets will exceed the data created in the developed world. In other words, if you and your company are not seriously invested in communicating online and making great use of all technological advances, you will simply be left out of the conversation[18].

The trust, which must be built between people doing business, is built differently in this new culture. Since we no longer get to meet the people with whom we do business, we must form our impressions of them, and their trustworthiness, in other ways.

A good reputation, as is evidence by reviews and endorsements posted on sites like Foursquare, Google and TripAdvisor by others who have used a business or service before, becomes valuable

---

[18]   Gruener, Wolfgang. *Global Data Volume Grew to 2.8 Zettabytes in 2012*. (2012, December 4). Retrieved August 15, 2015, from Tom's Hardware: http://www.tomshardware.com/news/data-internet-Global-Volume-Zettabytes,19728.html

currency in the new culture. Such reputation and earned trust allows this new way of doing business to succeed.

One example of where we must take the word of someone online whom we have never met is when we do business within what has been dubbed "The Sharing Economy". Here people rent things from each other (from hotel rooms on Airbnb to cars on RelayRides) by-passing the corporate middleman, and such companies are growing at a breakneck pace. Such "collaborative consumerism", as the consumer peer-to-peer rental market is known, was recently valued at $26 billion and shows no sign of slowing down— demonstrating, yet again, the internet's value to consumers and the need for a framework to be in place to help the consumer feel safe about trusting someone they've never met. Recommendations, ratings, reviews, critiques and references, all available online, serve as that framework and the younger workers and consumers have grown up with that being so. [19]

Technology, Communication and Sharing

Technology is the key that unlocks the potential of the perfect market for work. Because of the internet and hi-speed global wireless services and such communication platforms as Skype,

[19] *The rise of the sharing economy.* (2013, March 9). Retrieved August 20, 2015 from Economist.com: http://www.economist.com/news/leaders/21573104-internet-everything-hire-rise-sharing-economy

YouTube, instant messaging, Dropbox and GoTo-Meeting, geographical boundaries are no longer a hindrance to people working together. Such technology also allows education to be accessible to almost every person on the planet and technology will only continue to evolve—becoming faster, cheaper and more accessible, realizing the dream of one true global village. A company will be able to work with people from all corners of the globe on a project from all cultures and educational backgrounds. Diversity will become the norm, not just a vague byword in a company's HR manual. True talent, skill and experience will be the reason someone joins a project team—not just geographical proximity. Also, as we examined above, virtual meetings between people and establishing trust through reputation as currency will change the very way business is done and the types of businesses that are formed in the future.

Mindset/Culture

Such a change of culture will seem an organic change to those who grew up in Generation X or the Millennial generation. Look first at the concept of virtual work. The idea of working with others via technology, no matter where they are located geographically, even from different countries and cultures, was born and fostered online. Such virtual worlds are the younger generation's Mother's Milk.

The idea of IBM's "Big Blue," where only white American males were hired and even told to dress alike in the signature blue shirt and tie and where company-speak was rewarded with a lifetime of work in one place and a gold watch upon retirement—that is the true alien world to the younger people entering the workspace. A 25-year-old playing a virtual reality game online with someone in Svalbard, Sweden and working out how best to team up to build a city or storm a citadel—that is the natural way of doing things to them and they take such expansiveness with them into their new job.

He or she will find it a natural thing to be introduced to, work with, trust and give their business to people whom they have never met, nor are likely to meet. Technology is to these young workers as gravity is—an intrinsic part of their life, everypresent, constantly used and rarely thought of unless it were to go suddenly missing.

According to a Pew Research Center study, 75% of Millennials have created a social networking profile, 62% use wireless internet away from home, a full 88% of them use a cell phone to text (an activity 80% of the have done in the last 24 hours and which 64% of them confess to doing while driving.) In 2005, only 7% of people used social networking and by 2010 that number had grown to 75%—almost the exact percentage of Millennials who believe that new technology makes life easier. Tellingly for a generation who shun the old model of face-to-face meetings, 54% of Millennials believe that technology brings people closer together and lets them use their time more efficiently[20].

Organizational Structure

In the future, companies will let go of such structural hierarchies—and the role of management will be completely redefined in the new networked organization. This type of organization, that does not rely on hierarchical, complex structures anymore, but on distributed, simple networks that regulate and manage themselves, is the last ingredient that makes the future of work as envisioned in this book possible

Now technology and the way Generation Xers and Millennials view their slot in the workplaces of the future (from hierarchical to networked) makes space for new models of work to be applied— much more flexible, more bottom up than top down. This allows for increased use of technology and to make better use of the virtual talent coming in, highly motivated to accomplish that specific task. This allows for companies to get their tasks done with correct talent and within a tight timeframe.

That job, also, is very probably not going to be the one they have for their whole career. In the

20   Pew Research Center. *Millennials: A Portrait of Generation Next.* (February 2010). Retrieved December 24, 2015, from www.pew-socialtrends.org: http://www.pewsocialtrends.org/files/2010/10/millennials-confident-connected-open-to-change.pdf (PDF)

new networked organization, the workers of the future economy expect to work at different tasks, on different projects, in different places whenever they like. The idea of a boss, set hours and reduced opportunities is a thing of the past in their eyes.

Already today some companies are experimenting with the idea of a company without hierarchy or a formal boss. Later in the book we will look into two examples and the way they resolve issues of organization, process and decision-making in a complete networked organization without formal hierarchical structure. They are very good examples of what we will have to expect for the future

Such manager-less companies will soon become the norm as companies streamline their process and strip their organizations of unnecessary deadwood. Millennials, 95 million strong at present and who will comprise 75% of the global workforce by 2025, may never have a job in a traditionally organized company. They will take their place in the newly structured companies or join the ranks of non-traditional workers, like the 53 million freelancers currently working today. With nearly a quarter of the population in the US, UK and Canada already engaged in some form of economic sharing, collaborative consumerism and the Sharing Economy is here to stay.

We are beginning to see such changes beginning in company cultures. As we add more virtual workers and adapt new concepts for creating value, companies will experience a quantum leap in innovation. Combined with the undoubted increase in productivity afforded by the changes in the new workplace, gains will be astronomical and our economy will benefit. Since they will choose their own hours, workers quality of life will greatly improve. As they are their own bosses, workers will be truly motivated to excel.

Workers who have taken responsibility for their own work and get to make full use of their education, experiences and talents; companies who have the skilled help they need to improve and innovate; making better use of continually evolving technology; as well as improved communication, sharper focus, less overhead and higher profits for companies the world over—these are the components that will finally fix what once seemed unfixable—the broken market for work—and with this we will finally answer the $500 billion question.

CHAPTER SIX

BUILDING BLOCKS FOR THE HUMANCENTRIC ORGANIZATION

"Tomorrow belongs to those who prepare for it today."

—African Proverb

As we rush headlong on to that second half of the chessboard, with the online generation coming of age and hard on our heels, we are going to need new organizing principles and they'd better be both dynamic and flexible—because, when it comes to the future of work, time truly does wait for no man.

It is time to change our brains. We have to think differently about organizations, processes, hierarchies, companies, job descriptions, work, employees, compensation, and appraisals, and get ready for the adoption of humancentric organizations and even a more humancentric society. We start with some basic building blocks upon which we can build even the most complex organizations.

But for this new paradigm to work, every element must be holistic—built to work in harmony with every other element, whereas today, what we define as "work" is too-often drudgery. Tomorrow that drudgery will become job satisfaction. What we know as dry and lifeless "output" will become shared success and both these outcomes may be credited to our use of flexible and adaptable systems, which will respond seamlessly to new challenges.

I see three main categories that need addressing before we reach are able to transform today's corporation into tomorrow's humancentric organization and to let us build the organization that allows for the perfect market for work:

- **Organization Of Work:** What we today call structure or processes, that pyramid under which most businesses operate with the boss at the top and everyone else slotted into place below.
- **Communication/Collaboration:** This refers to the operational area of today's businesses, usually the purview of middle management in a traditional organization.
- **Evaluation/Incentives:** That for which we work today—salary, incentive plans, stock options and other motivators—mainly driven by Human Resources.

We need to take each of these old concepts off the shelf, give them a good shake and blow the dust off before we can make proper use of them. In the following paragraphs, we try to square the circle between the concepts and definitions as we know and understand them today, and how they will change in the future of work. These concepts are, in many cases, not appropriate for the humancentric organization, but we believe referencing them helps define what they will mean in the future. We will only briefly touch on each as discussion of any one of these concepts could fill an entire book.

Organization of Work

"Nothing is less productive than to make more efficient what should not be done at all."

—Peter Ducker, management consultant, educator, and author.

Too many cooks really will spoil any broth, so to get any job done, work has to be divided up and a certain level of organization imposed. In a traditional organization, tasks are divvied up and assigned to one team member on a permanent basis.

If the new brochures have to be created, the task falls to the marketing manager and everyone else washes his or her hands of the task. After all, she was hired to do this job. It is in her job description, not to mention she has spent her time with the corporation learning what type of information needs to be in the brochure and how that information is to be phrased. She has had countless meetings with stakeholders who have input into the brochure and had the IT department create a software program to template the brochure and create a contact list for the prospective customers who will read it. She has scheduled a seminar with every in-house department to go over the new products to be described in the brochure. If new employees are hired, she will repeat the seminar and that is about as adaptive as her job allows here to be and, should she get hit by a bus, it is up to the company to hire and retrain someone new. Her replacement must basically reinvent the wheel. Everyone from management and IT to internal communications and human resources—expending time, money and intellectual treasure to begin all over again. This top-down approach demands a high investment in organization, coordination, and communication.

In a humancentric organization, however, this concept is turned on its head. Every member of the company is part of the effort to not only create that marketing brochure, but make sure it is the best brochure that can be made. Tasks are assigned, to be sure, but everyone is kept up-to-speed on all parts of the process, so anyone can fill in for anyone else. There is no Broadway star in this performance; all are understudies, ready to take the stage at a moment's notice. "The play's the thing," Shakespeare said. Here, in the humancentric organization, the common goal is the thing and such common goals are the future of work.

Structure

Even in the bright new humancentric future, structure is vital to efficient work—without it, tasks are amorphous and the people working on that task are hindered by fuzzy focus. But what is meant by structure in the new paradigm I am proposing is as different from the current structure as night is today.

In the humancentric organization, structure won't be imposed by hierarchies, seniority or even job description. Structure will be established by the needs of an ever-changing environment. Individuals will be added to a team when needed and leave when their task has been completed—like ringers on a baseball team.

Let's take the example of our marketing director and her brochure project. Rather that have her source, price and arrange printing of thousands of brochures to hand out at a trade show, a printing specialist, one fully conversant with paper weights, cost per thousand, print-run timing and shipping parameters may come onto the team long enough to sit with the graphics department working on the brochure, He will advise the graphics team that a four-fold brochure of a certain size is the best, that the bar code needs to be in a particular spot on the outer edge, help secure the postal code required, supply it to the graphics team and they can design the brochure accordingly. Then the printing specialist can leave the team, saving the corporation the cost of paying for their specialized expertise permanently, when it is only needed temporarily—with no need to train the marketing director in this facet of the project.

For that matter, the graphics team can also be comprised of independent workers—not permanently attached to the company. This team can be called upon on a per-project or contractual basis to work for the corporation, but remain independent entities—allowing them to work virtually and saving the corporation training time, office space, benefits, and the responsibility to keep the graphics team employed full-time. They are free to pursue other work.

This more flexible and adaptable structure also allows for independent workers to work on a task though they are physically located in different geographical places and times zones and may even be part of a different culture or speak another language. As is already commonplace with the integration of independent workers into project teams, this concept will advance many steps. This literally opens up the world to the corporation who may now make use of global talent and such use needn't be limited to one-up work or a single project but may be tapped for any kind of intellectual tasks that present themselves to the corporation.

The new structure will come from groups of people coming together—whether permanently or temporarily –to work for the corporation:

Insiders: Like people employed today by traditional organizations, Insiders are individuals strongly linked to an organization, who have earned a high degree of trust within the organization and have superior insider knowledge of the organization's products and services. From a human resource perspective, Insiders are the individuals in the new structure who most closely resemble today's full-time employees. It is this group who will create core competencies, develop the corporation's business model and grow the company over time.

They will have some contract with the company, whether this is a full-time employment contract or a per-project contract or even just a loose retainer, reserving their time and paying them even when their services may not be required at that exact moment. They may have special privileges within the organization and special access to everyone affiliated with the company—even, say, the board members— or permission to view classified materials. The Insiders will limit their activity with other organizations and either come trained or the organization will train them, giving them the specific know-how they need to do their jobs.

Trusted Members: Trusted Members are those people who make up a pool of individuals that has been prescreened by the organization and may be called upon to support tasks within the company immediately and without the need for approval. They have already been approved based on their capabilities, satisfactory job performance and cultural fit. This group will also count, among its numbers, former employees. They have an open-ended contractual agreement on file with HR. During their previous work for the organization (and other organizations), these people will receive good evaluations and high recommendations, letting the organization see that they are placing their faith in people who deserve to be deemed "Trusted" Members.

Trusted members will have the job skills and capabilities that will help complete the task required by the company (and may even be allowed to know the "trade secrets" of the company for which they are working at the time. They will be constrained not only by confidentiality agreements, but have displayed the integrity necessary for each corporation, in turn, to trust them and highly recommend them to the next organization. For them, their reputation truly is everything.

These Trusted Members will be guaranteed a certain number of ongoing tasks (and money for performing them) for the corporation, but will not have a guaranteed minimum income. More tasks can be undertaken for the corporation as the projects progress, which will change the amount of money they can make, and they will also be free to offer their services to any other organization (with the exception of direct competitors) whenever they are available.

Trusted Members in Evaluation: They either were once Trusted Members, but due to long absence from the company, substandard evaluations or failure to keep up with the latest training, they lost their Trusted Member status. Or they are new members, who haven't worked with the organization before, but are proposing themselves to become Trusted Members and are willing to get the training, do the quality work necessary to get higher evaluations and make themselves available to put in the time to gain the trust of the organization. Every company will set its own criteria designating the various hoops such a prospective member will have jump through; which background checks need to be performed, what training will be required, what type confidentiality agreements and contracts will need signing and how long the period of evaluation will be, but always, the most important facet of this process will be the peer evaluation given by the other people with whom they work on tasks within the corporation. These proposed members will be judged, literally, by a jury of their peers.

Ad hoc **Members:** Many of the non-strategic, standardized tasks, like list compilation for marketing or a call center for level one screening of customer complaints, can be outsourced to Ad Hoc Members. No complex training program is required nor any classified information accessed. Insider knowledge of the workings of the company is not needed and only minimal supervision is needed. These Ad Hoc Members can offer their services to the corporation as individuals or other independent small businesses can organize the needed workers and offer their company to fulfill the task at hand. Again, though, a company's choice to hire an Ad Hoc Worker or group of Ad Hoc Workers will be based on the evaluations they present.

Which people (and how many) from these groups will form the structure of the organization will differ company to company and the tasks on which they work will by market forces and the decisions made about those by the Insiders.

But no matter what structure is in place at any given moment, certain tools will be needed to manage the resultant structure. Proper management will be needed to:

- Evaluate members based on their skills and competencies, their past performances records, their network connections and reviews and the level of trust based on those items
- Find and select the right individual for the task at hand.
- Determine incentives to reward the individual performing their part of the task as part of the team.
- Establish and make transparent the interconnections of the different tasks.
- Discover and use relevant information and tools to complete the tasks in an efficient and complete manner.
- Collaborate and make use of communica-

tion tools to seamlessly work together independent of geography, language, or culture.
But what if that oversight needn't come from traditional managers? What if technology and this
paradigm about the future of work, rooted those
bigwigs from the executive suite and made the
oversight of tasks easier, quicker and cheaper,
while still guaranteeing that the project came in on
time and under budget.

I had a fascinating discussion about this topic
with Kevin Fidler, who heads the Workable Fu-
tures Initiative at the Institute for the Future.

The Institute created prototype software named
"iCEO." As the name suggests, iCEO is a virtual
management system that automates complex work
by dividing it into small individual tasks. iCEO
then assigns these micro-tasks to workers using
multiple software platforms, such as freelancer
platforms, Uber, and email/text messaging. Basically, the system allows a user to drag-and-drop
"virtual assembly lines" into place, and run them
from a dashboard.

They ran an experiment where a report was
prepared using iCEO, which routed tasks across
23 people from around the world, including the
creation of 60 images and graphs, followed by for-
matting and preparation. QA and HR were also
automated by iCEO. (The hiring of UpWork contractors for this project, for example, was itself an
UpWork assignment.)

The results were stunning. Where it was anticipated that the research alone for such a project would take weeks, it in fact took only three days and the full report, which was estimated to take months, was completed (and of the highest quality) in only a few weeks.

It seems that, in the new humancentric model of work, those indispensable senior managers are not so indispensable after all.

Task Management

Tasks can range from tiny micro tasks to huge projects conducted in combination with many teams and even machines. They may take a minute or the combined effort of hundreds of people for a year. Some tasks are standardized and repetitive, whereas others are unique or even one-time events.

But all tasks share common characteristics. Each has a defined mission (decided upon by Insiders, stakeholders, customers or the market itself). Each has a desired outcome. Each requires a measurable amount of time and needs certain resources (be that manpower or machine or a combination of both) to complete its mission successfully.

Key tasks every organization will have are:

Strategic Management: Based on the competitive advantage, unique competencies, innovation potential, markets, financial situation, and ownership priorities, the strategic management's task is to create an environment capable of fulfilling the stated mission and achieving the desired outcome, spending the least amount of time, money and intellectual treasure as possible.

Proper Representation: No matter who is doing the communicating—a designated spokesperson, marketing director, sales executive or, communications representative specified by the organization—that person must properly represent the task to stakeholders and customers.

Tool Oversight: Each individual contributing to completed task must have access to various tools needed to bring that task to a successful end. Access to such tools will need to be managed and the security of any sensitive information must be guaranteed.

Tasks will obviously differ from organization to organization, but no matter what the task, they must be managed (mostly by Insiders supported by technology) to ensure efficient and effective task fulfillment.

It is also true that tasks are not static, defined once and for all and never changed. Tasks will dynamically change over time (lest the organization becomes fossilized.) Both task givers and task takers will adapt tasks depending on changes in the dynamic environment, information gained during the process of completing the task, insights gleaned by members of the task team and shared via the network.

Shareholders

For the last few decades, organizations' managers have become increasingly myopic. Their short-sightedness leads them to devote all their resources to making the bottom line look good for the next quarter or an even more frantic timeline—to raise the daily share price before the closing bell.

Such hyper short-term goals to satisfy voracious shareholders and add some zeros to a manager's bonus check, doesn't bode well for business in the long-term.

Investments with less than immediate returns become less attractive and it becomes a game of mergers and acquisition to keep up the frenetic pace. Money changes hands as quickly as a back room crap game and solid business goals are thrown over for what has literally become a gamble.

Such reckless behavior in the pursuit of the Almighty Dollar has led to a division between what the stockholders want and what the employees need. Those who actually produce the work increasingly complain about stress and ever-decreasing job satisfaction. Workers searching for more time with their families and to pursue other interests conflict with the narrow perspective of executives who too often think their employees should work harder, faster (and for less money). Such a disconnect leads to wasted time and talent, inferior products, missed production schedules, lost profit and much tension on both sides of the equation.

In a study conducted by France's Sociovision Cofremca in 2004, a whopping 75% of respondents agreed with the statement: "The interest of companies is usually opposed to the interest of its employees". A humancentric organization model would change this percentage by making use of dynamic and flexible structures and by redefining goals and desired outcomes. New funding concepts (which we will examine further below) would take the "heat" off of the need for ever-higher profits and ever-tighter margins, allowing room for innovation in place of strangulation.

Organizations clinging to the old ways will end up having a competitive disadvantage against other organizations in the marketplace. Organizations, who are completely aligned in their interests between the goal of the organization and the goal of the individuals trying to achieve those goals, will have a great competitive advantage.

Funding

Author Mason Cooley said "Money is Power at its most liquid" and that is certainly true when it comes to funding a business.

Bountiful financial resources are the basis of today's economy and will be the basis of the future digital age—whether those resources come in the form of greenbacks, Euros or bitcoins.

Funding is the grease on the wheel of commerce, making it possible to hire the right people and make use of the proper technology to finish those all-important tasks. Getting such funding through capital markets, bank loans and private equity will still be available in the new future I envision.

But other means of funding the organization will also evolve, like those now growing exponentially like crowd funding and member funding, as in today's Kickstarter, where people decide to throw their support behind a product or service they want to see come to fruition and through such (usually small) infusions of cash—add up to enough funding for the organization to meet its goals.

It is even possible that people will donate their time to complete a task together, pro-bono, with no cash payment at all, because they believe in the product or service being created. (The company's good reputation—established by the aforementioned endorsements and recommendations—becomes invaluable here.) By their donations filling up the company's coffers and providing the necessary funding, donors become a type of Insider themselves.

Corporate governance rules must, of course, be in place, no matter what form funding takes in the future of work.

Organizational Culture

Many companies today put a strong emphasis on a unique organizational culture, which is imposed from the top-down on to the lower rungs of the organization. Human Resources usually considers itself to be the guardian of the company culture and will employ people (specifically for specialist and management positions) based on the perceived cultural fit. Human Resources will also promote or penalize employees depending on their cultural behaviors. Only a few years ago, in order to become an executive, there were some pre-requisites other than your job performance. You had to male and white and probably hail from the right alma mater. Where I grew up in Switzerland, this delineation was even more specific. You had to have matriculated at the University of St. Gallen and have been an officer in the Swiss army.

Today that is different. In the more dynamic, flexible, and self-organizing structure of the humancentric organization, membership will be much more inclusive and less restricted than in today's traditional company.

People will have more varied backgrounds, may in fact come from other countries with different cultures, and perhaps not even speaking the same language. Acceptance of such diversity will be a given, People may spend only a limited time working on tasks for an organization. They may never in fact come into physical contact with any other member of the organization and work remotely, only connecting to the organization through virtual tools. Nevertheless, everyone will work with an eye towards, and respect for, the organization's stated values and goals, as there will be a strong incentive for common values and norms. All will be working for those positive evaluations of their work from Insiders and their colleagues, whether they work side-by-side with them or are only virtual coworkers.

In this organizational structure, reputation is paramount—the most important currency of all. These won't be the empty endorsements of the LinkedIn of today, where strangers can rave about the customer service talents of someone with whom they have never actually done business, nor the padded recommendations of a Yelp written by a business owner about their own company.

Is this system foolproof? Of course not, as every system is prone to some error. A jealous coworker may leave a false negative evaluation or a worker himself may delete all but the most glowing evaluations, but these manipulations should be readily apparent when weighed against other evaluations of the person and by application of a little common sense.

In the humancentric organization, workers will undergo a much more thorough evaluation by coworkers and managers and their perceived trustworthiness and eventual membership in the organization will depend on these evaluations.

Unlike in today's organization, where HR and perhaps a few managers get 30 minutes or so to interview a job candidate and use that short time to determine if that candidate is the proper one to hire to work for the organization for years to come.

In the humancentric organization, feedback is constant (allowing the worker to correct their actions and allowing the managers to make a change if necessary.) Candidates for Trusted Membership who can't or won't make necessary changes or who receive repeated negative evaluations won't be considered for future tasks and their general reputation will be impacted.

Workspace

Cubicles didn't come into being to crush the souls of the people forced to work in them. In the 1960's, some bean counter somewhere decided they would provide the best use of space and help employees keep their eye on the job (and not on each other) — saving the company time and money. What in fact happened was that the employees confined within such little boxes made jailbreaks to meet at the water cooler at every opportunity for a little human contact.

Earlier in my career, I had a meeting at a large corporation whose plant was situated in one of the most beautiful locations in North America. I was ushered into a glass-enclosed conference room, with a breathtaking view of the surrounding trees, where a few top executives awaited me. The other participants joined the meeting by conference call via the single phone in the center of the table — *from their cubicles down the hall.* They didn't even get to glimpse such breathtaking scenery from where they sat. It reminded me of the Greek legend of Tantalus, condemned to an unslakeable thirst while standing in a vat of water, the level of which would recede whenever he bent to take a drink. Satisfaction was so close and yet so far away.

Over the years, I have met plenty of executives, once the best and brightest of their generation, who fled to early retirement or continued on at their companies, stashed in their cubicles, until their enthusiasm for the work faded as surely as the light in their eyes.

Today with the trend towards working remotely, from home (or even the car), employees hold meeting by conference call, its true, but such meetings are very short in duration and most people use the time to multi-task, whether working on another part of the task or making bread, while listening in on the meeting. A repairman "attended" his weekly meeting with his manager (whom he had never met) via cell phone while fixing my cable the other day.

Such off-site work requires personal responsibility, dedication and good social interaction skills in order for such a collaboration to work.

Some tasks, obviously, will require workers to show up physically somewhere, but for many tasks, a virtual space will work just as well. Or a combination of the two might be required.

Managers may ask to meet their team at the beginning of task and only at specified intervals thereafter, saving those nonproductive commuting hours. In the humancentric organization, work hours will be flexible, not being dependent on a worker's physical presence, but on their work output. People may choose to work when they are most productive—meaning an early bird can still get in her predawn jog or a night owl write his part of the report at 2 am. A mom can catch her kid's soccer game and dad can make dinner for the family. Work hours no longer have to be limited to 8-5 and everyone doesn't have to aim to complete all his or her banking, shopping and car maintenance chores on the weekend, along with the rest of their fellow citizens.

Social skills and networking skills will become key elements for the success of an individual in the humancentric organization. A large, well-recognized virtual network will assure an individual's reputation. Everyone will be responsible their own employment and will need to add to, monitor and expand their personal and business networks to make sure they stay as fully employed as they would like to be. Social media tools like LinkedIn will evolve to accommodate these enhanced needs. No longer will you just sell yourself at the initial interview, get hired and wait for retirement. You will have to sell yourself and promote your capabilities constantly, which will give you new opportunities and assure that you remain at the top of your game.

Such hard work, ongoing education and experience gained will add to your reputation which in turn, underscored by favorable evaluations from those people and companies with whom you have done business, will be disseminated through your network and assure you future work.

Meetings

Meetings surely qualify as the biggest time wasters in modern organizations. Nothing has yet been found to take over their function of bringing parties together to exchange information, coordinate actions and provide necessary social interactions, though countless books and millions of dollars in consulting fees have been spent trying to improve them. Still, most employees or managers perceive meetings as counter-productive, taking time away from vital tasks, and would not attend meetings if given a choice.

I can't say as I blame them. In my career I have seen many managers organizing weekly one-on-ones and group meetings. In some cases, the manager had organized so many meeting with his team (individually and in different group formations) that he had not time for anything else—not even proper preparation for those meetings he had set up. Nor could the manager follow up on results from prior meetings, making every meeting even less productive than the last.

In a humancentric organization, meetings will still play an important role, but they will be held differently, depending on the purpose of the meeting. Meetings will have to be short — 18 minutes or less to accommodate the length of a person's attention span — and all meetings will be recorded. The recordings will be made available to other members of the organization right after the meeting has ended, so no one who needs the information will miss any key points. Even people unable to attend can either listen in live to the meetings or listen to the recording on their own time afterwards, perhaps while commuting or even working out at the gym. The recording will also serve to allow attendees to refresh their memory or hear again any points they may have missed in the meeting room. This also has the effect of holding everyone accountable for what he or she said and promises they made in that meeting. In the case of proprietary information, only scheduled attendees to the meeting will be allowed access to the recordings, which will be password-restricted as slide presentations currently are in SlidePoint, assuring a level of confidentiality — but an organization should aim for the highest level of transparency as possible. Many hands make light work, the old saying goes, and knowledge shared make tasks easier (and encourages new ideas and innovation) in the humancentric organization.)

Here are some of the types of meetings I foresee in the new organization:

Status Meetings: Today, these meetings are mainly used to report to management, ask for support, and to receive feedback. If these are scheduled regularly, often workers have nothing new to report or, if a manager needs up-to-the minute info, he isn't likely to be able to wait until the next regularly scheduled meeting. He either solicits the information by email or schedules (yet) another meeting.

In the new organization, most of these meetings can be scrapped and online tools, like Mavenlink, Clarizen or Workflow Gen will track everyone's progress and the status of the task at hand, making management reporting a thing of the past. .

Customer/Supplier/Partner Meetings: Nothing may ever take the place of one-to-one contact when it comes to sales. But such contact does not mean a sales rep must travel to Tokyo to bow to share a cup of sake with their prospective customer. Virtual meetings will be the norm (saving companies thousands in travel expenses and countless hours of time for everyone involved.)

Social media will become even more important as customer/suppliers and partners interact through Skype, email and workflow software (allowing for a permanent and correct record of all transactions.) As in all other areas of the new organization, the personal network of every individual and every organization will be the key driver on brand recognition, recommendations, and purchasing decisions.

Information Meetings: Internal and external knowledge databases, blogs, wikis, and social networks, will provide the lion's share of the information once shared at such meetings. Workers will share links to information needed for successful collaboration and search engines will provide the roadmap for searching out necessary research materials. A repository of knowledge will be created (by mandatory additions from all workers) and maintained by organizations–a library of information available to Insiders and Trusted Members, meaning no more reinventing the wheel with every new query. Experts, via internal and external blogs, will be available to question and receive the questioner will get answers. These Q&As and articles will be searchable by all members.

It will be like the Library of Alexandria was to the Old World, the repository of knowledge for the new organization

Decision Meetings: Whenever the organization needs to make a decision, which cannot be made by the individual, a decision meeting with *a* very *clear agenda* shall be held. There will be a short (less than 15 minutes) presentation by the person in need of the decision, explaining the background, the options, and the consequences of every option. A brief Q&A session will be held, with a decision being made the spot. Only when fundamental facts are missing can a decision be postponed and it will be strongly recommended that no one call such a meeting without having all the facts at hand. Wasting people's time will be considered a mortal sin in the new organization.

Coordination Meetings: Such meetings won't be needed anymore, as all coordination will happen with the team handling the task. Team members will search for input when needed and provide output as the task is completed. Using software and social media everyone remains "in the loop" all the time.

One-on-One Meetings: Used now by managers to stay in touch with or get information from their employees, these meetings are often spontaneous ("Hey Mack, can you stop by my office later?") and suffer from a lack of agenda. Because of this, the information exchanged is incomplete, neither person is ready to discuss a subject fully, and the topic will have to repeated during a future meeting where all team members are present—a classic waste of time. In a humancentric organization, these meetings will fall by the wayside.

Evaluation/Appraisal Meetings: The infamous Employee Review happens once or twice a year in most of today's organizations.

These are times of dread for the employee (whose wages are at least somewhat dependent on the outcome) and the manager, who has to come up with ways to praise and punish an employee without stepping on their toes and has to dredge their memory for examples of behavior from the last six months or a year for everyone who works under them. (This is usually preceded by a long stint of paperwork for the boss the night before the meeting and usually means only an employee's recent work gets considered in the evaluation).

Another problem with this type of meeting as it is now held is contained in that phrase, "working under them." All such Reviews are top-down affairs, with the boss reviewing the employee and never the other way around. Colleagues are rarely consulted at all.

What happens is the old schoolteacher solution; give everyone a passing grade—not too high and not too low—to avoid a lot of angry parents' phone calls. Every worker is marked "Average".

In the humancentric organization, feedback and evaluation happens continuously and is supplied by every member of the team, as well as customers, suppliers, and other partners.

Evaluation isn't limited to performance, but includes social and cultural components—a holistic approach. The whole person is considered—how they (historically and currently) play well with others, what talents do they bring, who do they know that can expand the organization's reach— are all considered in the evaluation of a worker.

Creative Meetings: Human creativity cannot be matched by a machine and technology. Adobe, Photoshop and whatever software tool will be used in the future, will always only be a tool to help an artist (whether they are a graphics designer or a copywriter) to create. Some creative collaborations will always be best handled in person and will take place, albeit irregularly, in the new organization. Others will be handled in cyberspace through use freelancer platform sites like PeopleAsAService and UpWork, for hiring independent workers like writers to handle text or create web content or sites like Onoise, an online marketplace for hiring audio professionals. Creative professionals will bring their own laptops with them to physical meetings and work with the tools with which they are most comfortable from their remote locations. Rarely will you see an on-site graphics department at a corporation in the new humancentric organization. Such individuals will have clients of many organizations while working for themselves.

Project Strategy Meetings: These meetings refer to a gathering (usually of managers) to give directions concerning the task at hand, based on internal and external factors; criteria that they, as top-down managers, now must impart to their subordinates.

In the new paradigm, all stakeholders are brought together, either physically or virtually, to throw out ideas, collate them, set directions, divide up the tasks of a project and leave knowing what is to be done and by whom. This type of meeting is held only at the beginning of a project. While the project is underway, status updates are handled via workflow applications.

Strategy Meetings: These meetings happen

maybe once a year (or less) to bring together all relevant insiders to discuss, evaluate and define the long-term strategic direction of the company and the tasks that derive from establishing that direction. Opportunities, risks and changing marketing conditions are discussed, as are internal challenges. Independent of hierarchy, these meetings allow all viewpoints to be discussed and considered and are the key to the future success of the company.

Social Meetings: It is good for team members to know with whom they will be working, but neither through just the cold exchange of resumes online nor over coffee and bagels at the nearest crowded Starbucks.

The smart organization of tomorrow will make use of professional networkers and team-builders experienced in facilitating such meetings. If possible, the participants may meet physically and the event will be structured to make the most of all attendee's time together, (no one will just be handed a disposable name badge and left in a room full of strangers to try and figure out who is who and who does what.)

If people are not in the same city (or on the same continent) short introductory sessions will be held virtually, via videoconferences between Insiders and other members, including those workers who will be new colleagues. Putting a face to a name will help team members work together more smoothly. Such virtual meetings may become the norm in the future.

Recurring Meetings: Almost every larger organization has a certain number of recurring meetings, some just to help define an employee's status. Managers-only meetings, for example, have much the same purpose as the old Executive Washroom key used to have—to separate the bigwigs from the peons. In the new organization, all meetings will be recipients of some hard stares and recurring meetings particularly. No meeting should be held just because that's the way things have always been done. Meetings, even virtual ones, should only happen when the situation demands it—not to share Danishes and gossip. All energy should be expended to getting the task completed. If a meeting doesn't directly serve that end, that meeting should be scrapped.

The Organization of Work

"Alone we can do so little; together we can do so much."

—Helen Keller (1880–1968), American author and political activist

One of the critical differences between us and the animals (besides that handy opposable thumb) is our ability to communicate complex content to each other.

Our friend, Og, any have been limited to grunts and gestures, but soon his descendants began stringing together words, then whole sentences, then expressing complex thoughts (which he soon committed to paper), before inventing the telegram, telephone, television, video and now social media from YouTube to Skype and the hundreds of apps that our keeping us connected. The need for humans to communicate with one another has never lessened and that communication has never been easier than it is today

Many of the new technologies introduced in recent years were focused on the private individual, and adoption rates for some of them have been phenomenal.

Conversely, in the business arena, new tools for communication have left only a limited mark, with their influence mostly felt in the B2C environment, augmenting traditional sales and marketing.

Let's look at what these new communication tools can do in business *outside* of the sales and marketing departments.

Social Technologies

Technology already has and will have even more strongly in the future, an important impact on the way social interactions will take place in business.

Key elements of the power of social technologies are:

- Everyone can create, share, and consume content and do so in their own time and from their own space. By expanding their network, the supply of such content is virtually limitless.

- Commercial interactions can become independent of intermediaries through the use of social networks and social concepts. Say farewell to the middleman.
- Networks will form as needed and will replace the traditional sense of what constitutes an organization.
- The use of social maps to manage influence and contribution of co-workers.
- The creation and use of Reputation as an online "currency".

Let's dig a little deeper into some aspects of these concepts:

Personal Reputation

In today's organizational world, the employer gathers information on the employee's performance for use in evaluation of that worker, influencing their wages incentive plan, and upward mobility in the corporation. Depending on a country's privacy laws, either more or less information on the person can be gathered. This evaluation process is one-sided (the company looks at the employee) and top-down (the boss, manager or the HR department does the looking,). The worker being evaluated has only limited control over what information the manager finds and the presentation of that information. The individual's shortcomings might stand out like the proverbial sore thumb in the presentation rather than his or her (often underutilized) talents. The person's aspirations, goals and dreams—much less her ideas about her job—are hardly taken into account.

In the humancentric organization, it is the individual who takes control of the presentation and partially of the content. Like Facebook does now for private presentations or LinkedIn for professional presentations, information on the worker will include more detailed descriptions of experiences, talents, ideas, and preferences and support those descriptions with blog posts, penned articles, tweets, past evaluations, endorsements and recommendations. A fuller picture of the person will be presented.

The person being evaluated will define different privacy circles for friends, professional insiders, acquaintances, networking contacts, and the general public. A profile will be searchable based on the privacy settings of the individual, and a ranking will be established making use of the quality rating of a person's skills, talents and experiences. Other search terms will be used to ferret out more recommendations and positive evaluations from highly-rated individuals. The more of these that turn up, the better the individual's rating will be.

The individual being evaluated will not have full control of his/her profile, however. Parts of the recommendations and evaluations will be unable to be accessed by the worker herself, Similar to a restaurant recommendation on Yelp or a product evaluation on Amazon, every individual participating in the open humancentric organization will receive ratings from people with whom he or she has worked or interacted. Professional success will be strongly linked to a positive profile, with many good recommendations and evaluations, and a large network of highly rated individuals. This is the network element. A person's wide network does not necessarily make him highly networked. The people in his or her network need to have high networking value themselves and the links need to be active in order to strengthen the network. Algorithms will have to be developed to measure the network strength of an individual.

The Pursuit of Information

We are all born with some instincts –we are scared of loud noises and falling— but with no real knowledge. Yet within a few short years we understand a whole spectrum of knowledge that it has taken humanity several thousand years to amass. We do this by building upon the knowledge base of the generations who came before us—information they passed along. Knowledge passed from them to us like a river with a current flowing in one direction.

In a humancentric organization, knowledge and information will be a two-way current. Today people consume information passed along from knowledge providers—parents, teachers, and experts.

In the future, all relevant information on any subject will be made available to anyone in search of it, with privacy settings protecting that information that can't be openly shared. Anyone working on a task in need of input will find the needed information available online.

If the needed information can't be readily found, the questioner will post the query online and a robot response with the information will be activated or an expert will respond his or herself.

In the humancentric organization, all company knowledge will be searchable in the same way as words for which we are seeking the meaning. We type in the word to Dictionary.com or Wikipedia and the information comes right up on our screen. The organizations of the future will have internal wikis and search engines (with trust filters to guard proprietary secrets) so that members of a task team will have immediate access to the information they need to complete their task. "Shared knowledge" will be the code phrase for the future of work

Input to Output Driven Management

Time is used to gauge an employee's output in today's corporation. Our very job depends on us being onsite for a full nine hours, even though it is apparent that not all of those hours are spent profitably.

In the humancentric organization, the time a worker spends on a task will be much less important. True, deadlines must be met, but assuming that they are, how well that task is performed is what counts, not how many hours a worker has devoted to the task. A release from such artificial time constraints frees a worker not only to coach Little League or hand out meals at the homeless shelter, but to make use of that greatest of assets to any corporation—his or her brain. Workers will actually have time to think and that makes room for innovation. Unshackled, ideas can fly free.

As has been proven in many studies, our brains do not work at peak performance for nine hours straight without rest. Concentration spans are short, and the capability to concentrate over longer periods of time is limited.

In a current office environment, we consider busy people to be productive. The individual who stretches back in his chair and stares at the ceiling for a while is considered to be rather lazy. The fact is, if we do not want just average performance, we have to give our brains the time to rest, allowing ourselves to perform better

Collaboration Tools

Today a wide variety of collaboration tools exist but their potential could be better exploited if they were integrated with other tools discussed here in the context of a humancentric organization:

Communication Tools: Basic communication such as text, voice, and video has to be made available any time, from anywhere by use of such technology as secure communication channels, shared data platforms, virtual whiteboards for discussions and other workflow components. Every individual in a humancentric organization has to be trained in the use of these tools and compelled to use them with his or her colleagues to assure that everyone is on the same page. (No circumventing the system with private emails or a quick face-to-face with the boss.)

Machine translation tools will support communication between members from different cultures, who may speak different languages, not only in written form, but also with simultaneous translation for voice conversations

Misunderstandings caused by language and cultural barriers, as well as plain crossed signals between coworkers will be reduced and efficiency will increase. Communication tools will not only help us to make a connection between people and groups of people more easily, but it will also vault the hurdles of understanding through automatic translation and interpretation.

Keeping An Ear To The Ground: In marketing, sales, product development, service, and other areas of an organization, active and passive "listening tools" have to be implemented to better understand customer behavior and interest, to generate leads, and to better understand the marketplace. Workers of the future will be the first line and tools will be developed to help them gather the information they need to better understand their customers and their needs. Team leaders will stress engagement to their sales and marketing staffs (and head off any disengagement from members of the team, bringing them back into the fold when they are in danger of straying.) Online tools and proper monitoring of social media (Facebook, Twitter, Instagram, industry blogs) will help a company hear what is being said about their products and services. Such data must be captured, analyzed and put to work by being shared with company team members and being used to adjust product manufacturing, service providing, customer service and even sales techniques.

Shared Platforms and Data: Every department and the workers therein of the humancentric organization has a need to share information, update, and revise common work in progress, in real time. As previously mentioned, either off-the-shelf workflow software, like Integrify, Agiloft and Kiss-Flow, must be used or a custom workflow software created for the organization.

Every team member must be fully trained on the software and use it to complete their work on the task with all results being transparent to every other team member.

Exception Management Tools: Usually, standard and non-standard processes that run through machine and human interaction, will behave as expected, requiring no human to verify that everything is running smoothly. But, since human error may have come into play in the creation of the machine in the first place, strong exception management tools must be used to identify exceptions and automatically trigger the required task to resolve the exceptions when they occur.

The Connected Individuals: Networking

In the upcoming digital age, networking far beyond our current understanding will be a key task of every individual who is active in society and business. Before the internet and the widespread adoption of social media, our networks were comprised of the people we had met through geographic proximity, school, work, clubs, or other social activities. We would not consider someone we had not shaken hands with to be part of our network.

With the advent of social media, this has started to change. We add new members to our networks every day—via social media and shared acquaintances. Many are people we have never met and we probably will never meet, except in cyberspace. Like-minded people will find each other and such mutual interest will help keep these relationships alive and active.

In most cases, the building of those networks is not structured. In the humancentric organization and society-at- large, networks will gain in importance and will be built actively. Every individual will belong to many different networks with different purposes— personal networks, business networks, networks for specific interests, networks with different expertise levels, networks and for members of clubs, churches or civic organizations.

The separation between one's professional network and private network will become increasingly narrow. Every individual within a network will be rated depending on factors such as the number of connections, the activity level, the rating of his/her connections, and the value of his/her input into that network. New tools will be developed for every individual to manage his/her networks in an efficient manner and to improve the visibility and the rating within the network. This, of course, is a two-edged sword. Whereas you can build positive reputational value through those tools, whatever has come online about you, your close family and friends might a trigger negative reputation. A teenager might today post funny (or incriminating) content about a friend (or enemy) and such a post might haunt him, coloring his future and how well received his next job application is or if he has a positive job interview.

Evaluation and Incentivization

"One of the great mistakes is to judge policies and programs by their intentions rather than their results."

—Milton Friedman (1912–2006), Nobel Prize winner for Economics

Even though many people might not believe it, given the universal grumbling that is the answer to the query, "How's work?" most people actually like the job they have and actually enjoy working.

Nevertheless, most people will claim that they work only for the money.

For many years economists have tried to give non-financial benefits a price tag, so they could use it in their micro economic models, but without much luck. Perhaps it is finally time to look at other criteria for what we value about our jobs—like work-life balance, a level of interest sustained and knowledge gained at our jobs, pride in work well done, and happiness at having contributed to a greater good, as opposed to only financial rewards. Maybe paying the mortgage isn't the only reason we work anymore.

New ways to figure fair pay for fair work will have to be created in the new humancentric organization. Getting paid by the hour won't work when one's hours aren't calculated. Pay per task or project will have to be developed, making certain that workers make enough to meet their financial needs while receiving result-based compensation.

Evaluation

The evaluation system in the humancentric organization fulfills a completely new role. It is not only to give top-down feedback every quarter or so, but it is also a constant feedback loop from all colleagues who work or have worked with an individual. It is the basis for Insider (or outsider) status in an organization, the foundation on which teams are built, and the lifelong, semi-public reputation profile of every individual. Part of the evaluation will be public and independent, and part of it will be private and can be influenced by the individual himself. Credibility will depend as much on status of the evaluator, as it will depend on the evaluation in itself.

Evaluation: Traditional evaluations may still be part of the overall evaluation process. These will be conducted by everyone working or collaborating with an individual and can be entered into the record at any time the evaluator thinks is best to provide feedback. This can be done often or in quarterly or yearly intervals if appropriate.

Recommendation: Recommendations will be a central part of the evaluation system and can be awarded for work well done, a winning personality, a special achievement or talent, or many other reasons, the value of the recommendation will depend on the evaluator's value to give recommendations for this specific area. An individual might be highly valued to give a recommendation on his/her expertise area, but the same person's recommendation for another area might be valued much less.

Skills: Skills, whether they be professional (awards and honors, languages spoken, special training received) or personal (climbed Mt. Everest, completed Red Cross disaster training) can be added by the individual, attested by others, and confirmed by experts in the field (which would have the highest value.)

"Likes": Every evaluation, recommendation or skill on a person's evaluation profile will be open to receiving "likes" or "dislikes." Likes will make a certain point stronger, dislikes weaker and these opinions will not be shared only every now and again. Feedback will be constant.

This counts for everything, your new project, your result, your photo of your new dog. Over time algorithms will be developed compile *all* that feedback from all sources and will convert this into something meaningful. For example, if you have lots of likes on your profile for a certain skill and you have commented on someone else's blog, generating many more comments on your comment, or if you have hundreds of Twitter followers, the algorithm will gather that information analyze it. If all your followers are your cousins or any group of the same people over and over, the weight of their evaluations will decrease. If you attract a mix of people unknown to you previously, the weight of their evaluation may be higher. If the people commenting on your performance are all captains of industry or US Senators, the value of their evaluations will be higher still. The algorithm will be able to sort all of this data once a certain volume of information has been reached.

The combination of the above elements will define the value of a profile and the positioning in searches, where the current status and the activity level will be taken into account. More recent input will be valued higher than older input. What used to be influenced through hierarchy and position will now be influenced through a worker's networks and level of competence.

Gamification

Most people are happy to spend hours sitting in front of their computer or tablet playing games like *Angry Birds* or *Candy Crush*, but call those same hours in front of the screen "work" and what was a pleasure become drudgery.

A decade or so ago, developers began making use of the passion for which people played online games by using many of the same competitive reward concepts (ribbons, accumulated points, ascending levels) and creating work masquerading as a game.

Not only did the games concept paper over hitherto boring business applications, making them interesting, but astounding results were reported.

It is not only the way we assign a job to a person and the way we compensate that person that will change. The way a job is defined will have to be done in such a way as to make the job as attractive as possible to the person who will perform it, thus getting the very best people to do the job.

In one example, top scientists and AIDS researchers, while trying to stop the plague of deaths the disease had wrought, were stymied trying to decipher a crystal structure for one of the AIDS-causing viruses called the Mason-Pfizer monkey virus (M-PMV).

The University of Washington's Center for Game Science collaborated with the Biochemistry department and created *FoldIt*, an online puzzle video game about protein folding.

Foldit utilized a game-like puzzle interface that allowed people from all over the world to "play" and compete in figuring out various protein structures that fit a researcher's criteria.

To everyone's surprised, with over 240,000 "players" registering for the game and competing viciously against each other, a solution to the structure of the M-PMV was found in 10 days, creating a major breakthrough in the AIDS research field.

Such gamification (and the resultant creative collaboration) is certain to be a vital component of the new future of work.

Training

Lifelong Learning has long been touted as the key to success and job fulfillment. With an ever faster-paced economy, global markets shifts, and the changes coming in the new humancentric organization, knowledge and skills will hold still more weight in the job market and the willingness to add knowledge and skills to one's profile will be a key element for success in the new paradigm.

Trusted Members outside of the organization will decide to undertake a task, based not only on financial reward, but on the opportunity a task offers for learning a new skill to add to their profile. The organization will have to present tasks that are attractive to individuals in this way also, in order to attract the best talent.

Continued learning will become part of everyone's responsibility if they wish to remain competitive in the marketplace. It will no longer be enough to finish school and then expect the employer to take charge of all future training. A person's willingness to learn new things and the initiative they show in stretching out to gain new knowledge and educating themselves will be taken into consideration in their recommendations. A worker willing to learn new tools, languages, enter a new field, add to their knowledge base and entertain new ideas will fare my better in the new flexible business climate than one who became calcified in their expertise years ago.

This new learning will not only take place in schools and universities. Online training, peer-to-peer exchange, mentorships and internships, cross-cultural exchange and old-fashioned apprenticeship will all allow easier access for the global workforce to share ideas and learn new skills so that every person may compete for the best tasks for which their experience, skill and education have prepared them—no matter where they are in the world and no matter what their age.

Incentive System

Many more elements will become part of the incentive plan in the humancentric organization. Pay-per-time worked, with perhaps a yearly bonus based on some kind of performance metric or evaluation, will make way for a more creative financial and compensation system.

Base Salary: Insiders of an organization will receive a certain fixed income to guarantee their commitment to the organization and to allow them a certain standard of living, independent of their current task for the company.

Result-Based Compensation: What the market will bear will be the measure of results based compensation. The successful completion of a project will have to be priced and every individual who was part of the team will share in the compensation. This compensation may be equal or unequal depending on everyone's task within the project.

For example, to create a weekly company blog on an annual basis, the graphic designer may be able to use stock photos he purchased and a Word-Press template to create the place where the company blog is to be inserted. That may take him six hours. To fill that blog with weekly articles for a year may take a copywriter 60 hours. These workers should be compensated differently. Wherever a direct market incentive is not feasible, an indirect performance incentive has to be developed and implemented, based on the goals defined at the beginning of the task and based on the changes implemented during the task fulfillment process. It has to be taken into account that the more complex a project, the more likely that thing may change during fulfillment of that project. Those changes have to be taken into account to evaluate the success.

Learning: The development of new skills throughout one's career will be crucial for a successful individual. Formal and informal learning targets will become part of the incentive system to motivate individuals to accept tasks and to develop Insider's knowledge that will be useful in the future for the organization.

Reputation: The tasks undertaken, the team members with whom one has collaborated and the organizations for which an individual has worked will develop a person's reputation. This reputation will be formalized in the evaluation system and will be visible in his or her profile.

Network: Some organizations and tasks will offer the opportunity to further develop one's personal network. The larger a network and the better the quality of the people within that network, the more attractive the task (and the organization offering that task) will be to potential workers.

Fun Factor: individuals will be more apt to agree to accept the tasks, work with the organizations, and collaborate with the colleagues that can promise a "fun" project. In this context, "fun" means fulfilling and challenging tasks, interesting people and a hospitable work environment.

Nonmonetary parts of the incentive system will gain in importance, and organizations will have to work hard to compete in the struggle to attract the best talent.

Only the organizations capable of combining all elements mentioned above into an attractive package will be able to woo the best workers and achieve the best results. Personal and professional fulfillment will become paramount in the humancentric organization and lead to a society with better systems in work, education, healthcare and public services, and a more engaged and innovative group of people, putting their heads together to come up with the sanest solutions to both businesses' and society's problems.

It can't come a minute too soon.

CHAPTER SEVEN

BUILDING THE PERFECT MARKET FOR WORK

If you are not willing to risk the usual, you will have to settle for the ordinary."

- Jim Rohn, entrepreneur

We've examined the history and some of the reasons for its inevitability; now let us create the perfect market for work. As we have seen, the ingredients are there, the potential is enormous, the time is right.

Let's being with a definition from an economist's view:

"...Perfect markets [have] profound political and economic implications, as many participants assume or are taught that the purpose of the market is to enable participants to maximize profits. It is not. The purpose of the market is to efficiently allocate resources and to maximize the welfare of consumers and producers alike. The market therefore regards excess profits... as a

signal of inefficiency, that is of market failure, which is to say, not achieving a Pareto optimum." [21]

For those of us who haven't studied economic terms, "Pareto optimum" means the perfect price has been reached; the perfect equilibrium between supply and demand. That is what a "perfect market" is about—the correct balance. This is to say that this the perfect market as seen through an economist's eyes.

But everyone is not an economist, so let me make it clear that when I use the word "perfect", I am not doing so in an emotional sense. "Perfect" does not mean looking only at the elements that would comprise a perfect market in an idealized world. Such an idealized world does not exist, nor does such a perfect market. We are still far from such perfection. Its inception may depend on perfecting human beings first and, in fact, is not truly possible given our human failings, but we so we begin where we are and work towards *perfecting* the market in so far as we are able to do so. While it is true that it would indeed have to be a perfect market in an idealized world in order to achieve all the elements we will examine below, we cannot hit a target (or even fall slightly short of it) without first aiming at it. The sooner we take aim, the sooner we can transform an ailing corporate sys-

---

[21]   Perfect market. (2015, July 16). In *Wikipedia, The Free Encyclopedia*. Retrieved 01:28, February 10, 2016, from https://en.wikipedia.org/w/index.php?title=Perfect_market&oldid=671781990

tem into a robust and healthy market of the future.

Below we look at the elements that would comprise a perfect market for work in an idealized world.

Elements of the Perfect Market

Low transaction cost: This element benefits both sides of the equation—the company and the talent. Whether through their own efforts or via use of a Trust Broker, a company has full access to all the talent out there and the talent themselves are fully aware of all jobs where they could best use their skills and experience. Only then has the perfect low transaction cost achieved. Due to the fact that the company has full transparency about all the talent available to them (or makes use of a middle-man who has such full transparency), the company is able to shrug off the excessive costs of locating a pool of talented workers; sorting through hundreds of candidates to determine which of those potential workers *might* qualify for a position; screening, running background checks on and interviewing them; involving all the stakeholders in the company who would have dealings with them; and eventually training the chosen candidate. When all this is finally accomplished, much time and money have been spent. In economic terms, time *is* money, so lots of capital has been squandered, as it is true that not every candidate chosen will "work out" from an employer's point of view, or that the worker chooses to stay. In the perfect market, such legwork to find the correct worker is handled for an employer, and, as workers may join the company on only a project basis (negating all standard employee costs), the result is dramatically lower transaction costs.

The same holds true for the talent, who themselves have full transparency about all the jobs available to them, either through their own efforts or via a middleman like a Trust Broker. The talent no longer has to expend their time and treasure identifying possible companies or projects that could make use of their talents and for whom they would wish to work. No more narrowing them down, researching, contacting and interviewing (sometimes with many layers of the company), negotiating pay, hours and how long each project will take only to find (at the end of many long days), the talent is not interested in the project when all the information about it has been properly flushed out. Perhaps their terms of employment are unsatisfactory or the whole process has taken too long and either the project has been changed or cancelled and the talent has wasted endless time spinning their wheels. In a perfect market, where we have a market economy wherein supply and demand creates the market, we let the market do the work and allocate the perfectly fitted talent to every job and the perfect job for every talent. The market will always find itself. It is perfect because it is self-regulating. Perfect company-talent marriages are contracted, which suits both sides well.

No wasted talent: The way things are currently done, when a position opens up, a company's HR department casts their net wide searching for candidates to fill that position. But whether that net catches the right fish is entirely too random. Talented and worthy candidates might never hear of the job opening (as that is dependent on how well they conduct their own job search, if, in fact they are actually actively looking at all). Or, conversely, those candidates might never have their resumes read by a human at all, but be screened out of contention by the autobot the HR department must employ to sort through hundreds of resumes it receives. For want of a certain keyword, an opportunity for the worker to find the job that fits their talents and interests is wasted. In the perfect market, a worker can have their talents discovered as their "reputation" will literally precede them and Trust Brokers will act as matchmakers joining the worker's talents with companies' needs—in a marriage that will satisfy both. Today economists believe that about 5% of structural unemployment (meaning talent didn't find the match of jobs to their skills) doesn't mean the market is inefficient. Rather, it is believed that such a percentage is normal in order to take inefficiencies in allocation into account. In a perfect market for work, the percentage would be much smaller.

No wasted jobs: The flipside of the unknown talent going wanting is the wasted jobs that are not filled with the right talent or not filled at all under the current system. An HR department posts a job opening and advertises it first throughout the company and then on aggregate recruitment sites and social media. But what if none of the applicants for that job are the right candidate, with the correct set of skills and experiences who happen to be searching for a job and available within the time frame delineated by the job posting? (It is, in fact, almost a certainty, that with transparency missing, any candidate found will undoubtedly *not* be the perfect candidate.) Thousands of such jobs go unfulfilled or are poorly filled in businesses every year and that leaves a company with four choices: (1.) continue to advertise the position, delaying the work associated with that position (2.) have someone already in-house fill the position temporarily, though their talents aren't specific to the job and such additional tasks may put an undue burden on the employee stepping up to the plate (3.) take down the posting and shelve the job or (4.) fill the job with a less than optimal worker.

A perfect market would allow an employer to write a brief description of a job and reach out, specifically, to those workers particularly suited to the position, no matter where on the globe they may be located, either by searching via reputation online or through a Trust Broker. Since such a worker even might just be brought on board on a project basis, even virtually from a remote location (taking into account that the company now has access to a global pool of talent), every job may be filled by the correct person.

Perfect price for every job/talent: In a perfect market, workers set their own price. If say a programmer sets his price at $25 an hour, he will attract those employers willing to pay that rate or, in the case of a Trust Broker, be matched with an employer who offers $25 an hour or more for the job that is proposed. The employer will pay only what they deem a position or project is worth and the programmer will only accept jobs that meet his price. Since the programmer is free to work for many employers on many different projects, he may even decide to add or subtract the hours he is offering to work and average out his price over those hours to $25 per hour. The programmer gets the money he needs and the company only spends what it can afford—thus the perfect price for both sides has been reached.

Obviously, prices will change depending on supply and demand of talent with certain capabilities (comprised of skill sets, years of specific experience, education and the like.) If a certain capability becomes the hot new thing (such as once was the case with computer programmers), prices will rise for workers in projects requiring such capabilities and new talent will move into this arena, until all demand can be met, at which time prices will return to normal levels.

These normal levels will depend on how much investment (education, experience, specific skill) goes into any capability so, in a perfect market with normal demand, workers with higher levels of education, experience and skill will always garner higher prices than those with lower education and less skills and experience

Market will automatically allocate right talent to right jobs: The perfect market does not mean eradication of HR departments, but it will provide vital tools to the search for job candidates. In today's world, an HR professional is reduced to a face-to-face meeting with a potential worker only after the exhaustive process of recruitment and screening detailed previously is concluded. In this meeting, it is up to the HR professional using sometimes a generic set of questions, to "get to know" the candidate well enough to form enough of an impression to pass him or her up the line. This is an imperfect system at best (as is evidenced by the large number of new employees who leave within the first year of a new job). In the perfect market, it will be a simple matter to find the correct worker for a position or project and "get to know" them though the recommendations and evaluations of others who have worked with them on just such jobs previously.

As an added layer of credibility, a Trust Broker will be able to recommend exactly the right person for exactly the right job as their stable of talent is well-known to them since they have worked with the talent on many (even similar) projects previously. The same is true on the workers' side. They, too, will be able to check out a company for its suitability to match their own interests and talents using evaluations and recommendation from previous employees, temporary or virtual workers. They also may make use of a Trust Broker who knows the culture of a company with whom they have worked before and recommend that company to the worker. The company gets the use of the talent it needs. The worker gets to use his or her talents in a position in which they are interested. That is the meaning of a win-win situation.

An additional element to be considered here is the time frame. In the traditional market everything is long-term—the search, the process and the commitment. In the future of work, commitments will be much more shorter term, which in turn means that the whole process can be compressed, saving time for companies and workers. The other benefit to such a shortened time frame for both sides is that the shorter the commitment, the more risks the company can take in choosing a worker for a project and vice versa. Neither side has signed up for a career-long commitment. Things can change with the next project. The company can hire different talent and the talent can move on to another company and their project.

Also, as I have noted, new demand will emerge based on supply. If pharmacies suddenly find themselves with a shortage of traveling pharmacists, the price to hire such a professional will go up. When that happens, the number of pharmacists seeking such a specialty or students training for it will increase, with the end result of having enough traveling pharmacists to fulfill the need, at which time the price will go down again until the normal level is achieved.

Such increased efficiency for companies allows them to improve their market position: As shown above, the perfect market will allow waste to be trimmed, time to be saved and work to be completed on-time and companies will "get it right the first time". This increase in efficiency will allow companies to get a jump on their competition and stay ahead of the game, especially over companies who cling to the outmoded older business model.

The company of the future

So given these elements, what might the company of the future look like?

Let's begin with the heart and soul of any company—its people. The company of the future will have trusted core employees. These people have earned their trust, demonstrating integrity, loyalty (perhaps through long service) and shown that they understand the necessity for confidentiality. They have core competency and the vision to develop the company's strategy further.

There will be three types of trusted core people:

1. Strategic employees whose vision and core

competency allow them to invent the future of the company.

2. Those employees with what could be called "core know-how". They are skilled in how to inform customers and keep them convinced of the value of the company and they can use this talent to leverage the rest of the organization as well.

3. Trusted employee who must remain in-house, as their job requires hands-on control.

This above is the "in-house team" (even if the company only employs remote employees) who creates the plans, set the projects, oversees the management of the company, and develops future business. They are usually full-time employees who may receive benefits, bonuses, stock options and other amenities of the company and upon whom the owner, board of directors, management or, in the event the company is truly "boss-less", those people on whom their colleagues rely. In the perfect market, as in the current one, such people are invaluable.

The future company will also make use of variable trusted talent.

This pool of people may either be on-site or work virtually. These people have worked with the company (and its trusted core employees) on other projects. By their good work, reliability and integrity, they are trusted to complete their projects well, enhancing how the company fares in the marketplace. These variable workers are known to the company from previous projects, but were originally recommended by the reputation they had achieved due to favorable endorsements and reviews from others for whom they had worked. Or they have been sent along to the company to meet their need for specific talent by a trust broker with whom the company is familiar. These workers can be called upon to accept jobs in the company of long or short duration. Some may stay for years, others for merely weeks, and may return again for other projects where their talents may be utilized.

A company may make use of flexible virtual talent, by dint of their projects, they are short-term. These workers come and go as needed. Though not necessarily low skilled, these workers are the most easily replaceable. The work they do may be repetitive or characterized by a relatively easy process of instructing them in the job's requirements or by the ease in which the work is delegated to someone new, or by a very high level of specialization. For example, if the company has need over the course of a year to find copywriters to create blog posts about the company's product line for the corporate website and one of the writers who has been writing for the company for a long time needs to take a leave, the company can find another reputable copywriter easily. The substitute need only be supplied product information, a list of topics already covered, the length and frequency of the blog and a style sheet to get started. The new copywriter's reputation can be checked beforehand by reading over her endorsements and testimonials or the company may employ a Trust Broker to locate such a person.

How future companies may be organized.

As companies of the future morph from hierarchical to networked organizations, self-organizing structures will come into play. All workers will be rowing the same boat, pulling together to reach an overall shared goal. This is already happening as was documented in a recent segment *Global Business*, a podcast on the BBC.[22]

In the segment "Companies Without Managers", the program looked at the growing phenomenon of business with no bosses, not much management hierarchy and lots of initial initiative.

One of the companies examined was Morningstar, a California company that processes more tomatoes than anyone else in the world and they do so with no corporate overlords. According to one employee interviewed, that means that every employee is responsible for himself or herself. It strikes him that in other companies who have supervisors, it means people don't trust their employees to do the work.

---

[22] Jones, Rosamund, producer. *Companies Without Managers*. (2015, August 24). Retrieved August 29, 2015 from BBC World Service Global Business: http://www.bbc.co.uk/programmes/p02yxbsb

Gary Hamill, a business guru, familiar with the company's setup, was struck by the fact that there is not a single executive and no top-down bottom-up mentality or supervision. Colleagues negotiate among themselves. Workers contract with people downstream saying for example, "I will load this many tomatoes per hour". That statement becomes their commitment, not to a boss, but to their peers. Hamill describes this company, with no managers, as one of the best managed in the world.

Someone who shares these views is Frederic Laleaux, a Belgian management expert who has spent a career coaching executives in large corporations. He found himself visiting one such company seeing everyone rushing around with phrases like "change initiative" and "mid-term planning" ever on their lips. He found himself clearly seeing the artifice of those terms and began to wonder how it could be different.

He knew some companies operated extremely productively without anyone being the boss of anyone. In his book, "Reinventing Organizations," he wrote that the same tasks still need doing, but managers aren't the best way to get them done. Laleaux advocated a new framework in a peer-based fashion was the way of the future.

How are pay raises and financial compensation handled in such a model, such as the one at Morningstar? Peers tell you, their fellow worker, what they think about how you work. You have a score. It goes in a package, along with a letter, saying you want a raise or a bonus and how much. That packet goes to the compensation committee, comprised of four or five people within the plant. These people are not voted on in order to gain their positions. They volunteer and then the rest of the workers basically "just agree" that they can have a seat on the committee.

How about disagreements handled at Morningstar? One worker explains, "If I have a problem with you, I talk to you. If necessary, I bring in a third person or even a group. Such autonomy positively affects the workers," We feel important and when we feel important we want to do a better job."

There are rules at Morningstar. Any person in the organization can make any decision, including spending the company's money, as long as they have sought advice from someone in the company with more expertise in the subject than themselves and those people who will have to live with the decisions. People who are often consulted in this way are recognized as natural leaders and their reputation rises. Reputation is the currency at Morningstar, as I have suggested it will be in the companies of the future.

In Poole, England, the BBC journalists found a traditional company that has changed its spots: Matt Black Systems, a small specialty engineering company. The owners, Julian Wilson, Jr. and Andy Holmes packed up there desk and left the premises, overthrowing an extremely hierarchical system put in place by Julian's father, Julian Wilson, Sr. He had come from a big company background and established the well-known, workers/middle management/quality management/upper management/executive team structure. When his son took over in 1986, he and his partner noted first that the company was letting its customers down in terms of product delivery. The products were always late. The duo also analyzed overtime. Most of the workers were getting time-and-a-half overtime pay for any hours over 37.5 weekly and were therefore delaying the products manufacturing to earn that extra money.

Wilson and Holmes took a novel approach to the problem. They told the workers that their next pay packets would contain the money they would have earned if they worked that overtime, without having to work the overtime, thus eliminating the hidden incentive to delay the product. Then the managers stepped back and moved their desks out. Within a short amount of time, the hours dropped and the projects sped up.

"People had to change their behaviors in lots of different ways. They had to order things in a more timely way," said Wilson. "We noticed that there was a complex dynamic between people and their managers. As managers stepped in, workers stepped out. So we shed managers and have none anymore. In reality now everyone is a manager."

Engineers can call on each other for help and support. One employee described his changed responsibilities saying, "I'm in control of all of my accounts, credit control, purchasing, dispatch, audit, and ordering. I'm responsible for everything. If a project is too big for one man, you can partner with someone so your relationship with your peers is very important".

Each business cell has its own profit and loss account to which pay is linked. If one cell is failing and it can't get its fellow cells to support it through a bad patch, it won't survive. It is as though each person is his or her own entrepreneur sharing one brand.

With this boss-less system in place, the on-time deliveries at Matt Black Systems are now close to 100%.

Gary Hamill noted what such a framework means to companies who make such a change, "We get the people who want to manage themselves, everyone else gets the rest. You have people solving problems no one asked them to solve, taking responsibility for themselves...and the companies [which do this] are much more productive."

The report concluded that most of us have been imprinted by business school or past jobs or former bosses to *expect* to work in a traditional company where we are told what to do, but this idea is quickly passing. (At Matt Black Systems, all of the old guard employees, those used to how things *used* to be run, have left).

The perfect market of the future makes little provisions for such hierarchal companies. A networked organization can be much more effective and efficient and, to a certain degree, every employee becomes an entrepreneur. Add to this the concepts we have discussed above on the future of contracting talent to certain jobs and you get a very powerful mix.

Let's see how two different types of businesses might look in this new perfect market for work.

Case Study: The Real Estate Company

This real estate company has a brick-and-mortar storefront in a prominent place on Main Street, USA and is owned by a Realtor who gets a percentage of every other agent's business who works for her. There are five Realtors on staff: One for commercial sales, three for new or resale properties and one devoted to foreclosures. Each Realtor has an assistant to help schedule appointments and organize and greet people at open houses. Each Realtor also has a desk and computer in their own cubicle—all paid for by the company. A receptionist greets walk-in customers. There is also an advertising director who places all the ads, three prospectors searching for customers who wish to sell their home or business or buy another, a social media person who updates the listings and keeps current Facebook and Twitter and a copywriter who handles brochure copy and blog writing. The office also has a notary public, an appraiser and a home inspector on staff. There are two secretaries to type, file and handle all contracts and documentation, as well as a bookkeeper to handle office accounts and property deposits. There is even an in-house handyman to help fix small property problems.

The company also deals with off-site vendors like the title insurance company, home insurance firms, banks, attorneys, home stagers, plumbers, electricians and house cleaners.

It is an impressive medium-sized company and an expensive one to run, which forces the company to accommodate a certain deal flow and number of sales just to stay in business, no matter how the real estate market fluctuates. The company needs a lot of new deals/sales, to afford the staff need a constant flow of business in such an inflexible structure. In the future market for work, however, by making use of flexible workers, if the market fluctuates and with such fluctuation, a certain amount of sales fall off and income goes down, such changes can be accommodated more easily.

Here is how that same office can be reorganized in the future market for work:

There is no need for a brick-and-mortar shop, as everyone will search for properties on-line. If face-to-face meetings are needed, the Realtor will meet the client at the client's own home, bringing a laptop or tablet with them (doing away with paper brochures). Realtors work for themselves, sharing a company brand (say Coldwell-Banker). For a percentage of their commissions, they make use of the services Coldwell-Banker will provide, such as prospecting activities, advertisements and access to the preferred vendors from appraisers to home inspectors. From Coldwell-Bankers' perspective, they may exchange the receptionist for a call-in service that answers their office phone off-site and disseminates the information via text, email or even call forwarding.

Prospectors are another off-site service with a team of people reaching out via social media and even, if required in an area of a less technically-proficient market, via telemarketing. Marketing, social media copywriting services are completed by off-site firms who act as subcontractors and may never meet the Realtors, but communicate totally on-line—showing layouts and copy for approval virtually.

Each Realtor becomes their own Notary Public and appraisers and home inspectors are individuals hired on a per-project basis. They can even be employed on a retainer, agreeing to work on so many properties a month or year. Freelance secretaries take care of all paperwork, sending it by a freelance courier who includes the Realtor on the routes of his freelance business. The bookkeeper, who must trusted, but not necessarily be on-site, can set each Realtor up with the software of his choice to record financial transactions (ensuring the company and the Realtor get paid properly) and collect the records and money from the Realtors himself or make use of one of his trusted employees to do so. He will handle the banking and the dissemination of funds. The off-site vendors remain just that—vendors and offsite. It should also be mentioned that "offsite workers" can in fact mean "offshore workers" and many tasks can perhaps be performed by totally qualified workers offshore for the best price available.

Everyone in this newly formed humancentric organization is aware of their responsibilities and the benefit of keeping the corporate brand alive, and, as each is acting as his or her own entrepreneur, has a stake in keeping everything flowing smoothly, efficiently and profitably.

If the ever-volatile real estate market changes, the company can quickly scale its operations (and the talent it makes use of) up or down, making marketing more guerilla-based.

Each agent can do work cooperatively when workflow dictates such cooperation or be "their own boss" making use of virtual freelancers or not, depending on how they choose to "run their business".

The company can move from x employees to y employees, downsizing the agencies' permanent payroll while getting the work done through use of virtual talent.

Study: The Construction Company

Let's take a small construction company engaged in homebuilding. Whereas now they may employ a marketing staff, a cadre of salespeople, building designers, estimators, architects, project managers, complete construction crews (excavators, site coordinators, roofers, carpenters, plasterers, painters, electricians, plumbers, granite experts, painters, tile layers, pavers and landscapers) as well as people who work with the county pulling permits, arranging inspections and the like, bookkeepers, accountants and collections agents, plus executives overseeing every department, in the work market of the future, they can trim much fat off of their bloated staff.

A trusted core of people will remain permanently—perhaps a talented designer or architect as well as some of the workers in the financial department. For the rest, marketing chores can be farmed out to freelance digital designers, web content writers, copywriters who handle brochure creation, television and radio producers, media buyers who handle writing and placing the ads using their own contacts and journalists who can write advertorial articles by the piece.

Salespeople can become their own entrepreneur, making use of the resources provided by the company (marketing aids, telemarketing, office services) or strike out and use their own skills to find and develop prospects, creating their own marketing materials and answering their own phone—allowing them to make as much money as they'd like, not held back by inflexible sales arrangements or division of leads by the company.

Project managers can be hired as freelancers and work on one or more projects as they choose. All components of the construction crew can be hired as trusted part-time workers (and may be used over and over again if the quality of their work suits the company. The reputation they have—and maintain through the vagaries of crew changes—will determine how often they are asked to work on the company's project.

For administrative tasks like pulling permits, tracking contracts and arranging inspections such tasks can be done by relatively lower skilled (and therefore imminently replaceable) freelance workers.

Opportunities for Talent in the Perfect Market for Work

The perfect market for work as viewed through an economist's eyes means that the right job will always go to the right talent with the correct set of skills and that the right demand will be present on all levels, —price, time, duration, location and trust.

For workers, this means that they will no longer be squandering their talent, imprisoned in a cubicle doing a job they don't want to do, are overqualified for and literally hate, watching the clock and praying quitting time comes soon. The perfect job or project is available at a price the worker has set and he or she can choose for whom to work, from where, for how much and for how long. Certainly some jobs will pay more than others and, based on market conditions at any given time, a worker may have to adjust their hours to make the kind of money they wish to make, but in a perfect market, the worker is in the driver's seat. They may choose their projects and be their own boss. Also talent with qualifications where there is more demand than supply will have more choice, than if there is more supply than demand. This is true for both low- qualified as well as high-qualified workers.

The perfect market will also provide fertile ground for new jobs to be born. Workers in the new perfect market will increasingly create their own jobs. A golden age of the entrepreneurs will be born.

Without the heavy burden of starting an old-fashioned brick-and-mortar company or the necessity for a large full-time staff, an entrepreneur can start her company on a shoestring budget; from anywhere she has a fast internet connection. She can work with talent on a per-project basis, expanding her knowledge base without expending thousands in capital while trying to get an idea off the ground. She will have easy access to online tools to experiment with her business model, test it in the marketplace before fully committing, refining her approach and product and launch her company globally at the stroke of a key.

That talent with whom our entrepreneur may work to launch her new company may hail from anywhere in the world. Whereas once there were locations in the world, particularly the developing world, where potential workers stood virtually no chance of gaining the education, knowledge or experience to compete in a global marketplace, the internet and mobile communications have changed that scenario forever. Now the entrepreneur may hire workers from nearly everywhere on the planet. Also, because geographic borders no longer act as insurmountable walls between us, new companies will be springing up from countries we never considered players in the global economy.

Think of it: If Steve Jobs had been born in Central Africa, he probably wouldn't have built Apple, not because of anything inherently missing in someone of Central African birth, but because he wouldn't have had the education or resources he needed to start his company. He wouldn't have been any less intelligent; he would just likely be herding cattle, just as his father and forefathers had done in order to make a living for their families.

Now what if that herder had access to the resources of Jobs? What would be possible if every person in the world used their talents fully, as say the people in the technology cluster of Silicon Valley or in biotech cluster in Boston are able to do? There would be created a global pool of talent from which companies could grab the best virtual talent, no matter from where they hailed. If all people on the planet could gain access to the education and technology they would need to put his or her talent to the best use of his/her ability, how many more Steve Jobs would be discovered out there? How, if given a chance to fulfill their potential, would they change our world? There is maybe only one person in a 100 million who combines all the talents of Steve Jobs. Twenty years ago, when Jobs was in his prime, there were perhaps only a handful of people with his talent who lived in places where that talent could be discovered and developed. If everyone had access to the conditions necessary for their native talents to flourish, there might be dozens of such geniuses discovered, no longer unseen in a shantytown, remote village or forgotten farmstead.

Putting the Perfect Market into Practice

For the perfect market the work, there has to be full transparency of all the elements to create the desired outcome for both companies and workers. Only if the company fully understands the capabilities, work ethic, reliability and trustworthiness of the talent they would like to employ can they make an informed hiring decision. For its part, the talent needs to fully understand the job they are considering undertaking, the skills and hours required, the company and something of its culture and whether they, in turn can trust the company to do right by them.

Since it is a wide world and companies don't

know every talented worker that they might choose to employ nor does every worker know what companies would make best use of their talents, a problem presents itself.

Neither side has either the time or the access to all the criteria needed for them to make an informed decision about the other. At present, both sides have to put in lots of time researching, imperfectly, the information they need to make the right decision.

We know the endless recruitment chase a company's HR department must undergo, but for talent the approach is, of necessity, even more haphazard. They may troll LinkedIn hoping that some of their connections can help put them in touch with a useful company contacts or try to cull jobs from message boards or industry associations or hope someone notices their Facebook page or blogging attempts. Or they need to rely on first-generation freelance platforms like Upwork and Freelancers. com where they may be competing with thousands of other freelancers, with their resume being buried under an avalanche of CVs from all over the world, from workers with various levels of skills, many of whom aren't even qualified to "bid" for the job. To research a company in whom they are interested, independent workers are reduced to gathering information from a company's own PR-heavy site or read disgruntled employees reviews on Glassdoor.com.

The information gleaned by both sides of the

equation in the above current scenario is not only time-consuming to obtain, frustrating as hell but also spotty at best. All that effort and there is still a big risk that no one ends up with what they need to make an informed decision. What is to be done about this enervating situation in the future perfect market?

Someone who takes the burden off both sides and provides a valuable service is introduced… the Trust Broker.

The Trust Broker

A Trust Broker is the middleman, trusted by both the company and the talent to join the two together in a mutually satisfying work relationship, lifting most of the burden from the shoulders of both parties to find and understand each other's needs and trust each other

As we've seen, when it wishes to engage a worker, the company must identify and clearly define the task or tasks at hand. It must determine what resources will be necessary to complete the project. It must set a timeline and a budget for completion, It must clearly define which tasks need doing and what type of workers, both internal core workers already on staff and temporary workers who will be brought in from the outside for a limited time, will be needed to complete those tasks. It must write a detailed job and task description and begin the search for the proper workers to fill those slots.

In a traditional company of yesterday, this is where HR would swing into action and begin the long and tedious procedure of posting job openings, soliciting resumes, setting up interviews, checking background and references and on and on in the age-old dance of how one filled a position in the old economy.

In the future, however, the trusted members of the company contacts a Trust Broker, a company who has the contacts with temporary and virtual workers all over the world, who can lend their talents and expertise to the company's prospective project. Such Trust Brokers differ from traditional headhunters, as they are not just offering to handle the endless steps of hiring a permanent employee and taking much of the preliminary resume and reference work off the shoulders of an HR department. These Trust Brokers know and have worked with thousands of temporary and virtual workers, locally and globally, and know, first-hand, the workers' strengths and weaknesses when it comes to a company's specific needs from having worked with the temporary/virtual worker on many other projects for many other companies. The Trust Broker can vouch for the worker's integrity, work ethic, talents and particular skills from having dealt, first-hand, with that worker in the past.

Naturally, this arrangement involves an element of trust between the Trust Broker and the company, as well as between the Trust Broker and the temporary/virtual worker.

A company who is looking to hire a virtual or temporary worker, knows very little about the person to whom they will be entrusting their project or task and have no way to quell their fears by investigation of the type they conduct when hiring their employees under the old system (checking job references, running credit checks, investigating education and licensing, etc.) They need to take someone's word for the quality of the employee—someone who has worked with the virtual freelancer and knows whereof they speak.

From a temporary/virtual worker standpoint, the issue of trust is pretty straightforward. The virtual worker is concerned, is he or she going to get the support you need? Has the job been well defined? Is he/she going to get paid, in a timely manner or at all?

Current employees of a company know who does what to whom, for good or ill, within the current company management structure. Virtual or temporary talent doesn't have that level of trust or knowledge about an organization. They must rely on the integrity and knowledge of the Trust Broker.

The Trust Broker on both sides of the equation, is a very important middleman between prospective worker and the company with a task that needs completion, so let's look at the role of the Trust Broker in more depth.

The Trust Broker reduces risk, time and cost and helps to make the market more transparent and therefore closer to that perfect market. Companies and virtual talent both will have to invest some time and research to assure themselves that they have chosen a reputable Trust Broker. In the Trust Broker's case, his "currency", a reputation for integrity and reliability, is what will earn him all his future business.

The Trust Broker may work with a virtual freelancer over a year's time and work with them on multiple projects. They become well acquainted with that worker, having had time to choose the proper people from a pool of thousands—eliminating the need for the company to do research and selection and negating the risk for the company.

This is not a classic case of the HR professional choosing five resumes out of thousands they received. In this time-honored system, the company is obligated to invest in research, background checking, interviewing checking the references of prospective employees. Such time, money and resources are invested whether the new employees work out or not. And many of them don't. Of new hires, an estimated 46% fail within 18 months. [23] So the company is out time and money and they still have to begin the process yet again. This is another reason traditional companies are in such bad shape.

[23] Schwabel, Dan. *Hire For Attitude*. (2012. January 23). Retrieved September 14, 2015 from Forbes.com: http://www.forbes.com/sites/danschawbel/2012/01/23/89-of-new-hires-fail-because-of-their-attitude/

In a humancentric organization, all employees aren't on-site employees. They are virtual talent, hired for projects only and for only days', weeks' or months' duration, and they are hired on the reputation their work with others, including the Trust Broker, has earned them.

Since the virtual worker's reputation is truly their calling card, they work from a different set of assumptions than a traditional employee. Let's look at an example to see the difference:

Think of your experiences with taxi drivers who are employees for traditional taxi companies. Your impression of the drivers may include such negatives as unreliability, dishonest dealings, language barriers and rude or hostile customer service. They are paid an hourly wage (plus some mileage) to get you from one place to the next. They may even get an (optional) tip and have been known to complain what they've been given isn't enough. Whether or not you ever call their bosses' taxi service again is of little consequence to them. They will work their next scheduled shift whether you call or not.

Now contrast that taxi driver with an Uber driver. Uber drivers are not employees of anyone. They are people who offer their cars and driving services to transport you in many American cities, and their market is growing. Why? Uber drivers are invested in retaining you as a customer, as opposed to just getting you where you are going. The Uber driver relies on his or her friendliness, cleanliness and reliability to ensure you will make use of the Uber app to request him or her again the next time you have a need for a ride. He earns his good reputation by favorable customer ratings and feedback. Such drivers have a motivation to be nice to you. Uber, the company, in this instance, acts as the Trust Broker. They have worked with these drivers time and time again and know what to expect of them. If one of the drivers transgresses against their stated company policies, is dishonest, rude or unreliable, or if the driver receives negative ratings and feedback from customers on the Uber site, they don't get to call themselves an Uber driver anymore. They have lost the Trust Broker's good opinion.

As in interpersonal relationships, trust is hard to gain, easy to lose and almost impossible to restore. In the new humancentric organization, trust is just as important and reputation is everything.

Since the people in the company doing the hiring have never met (and, depending on the project, may never meet) they must rely on not only the Trust Broker's word for the quality of the person they are considering hiring, they rely on the reputation of the worker his or herself. This reputation is evidenced in ratings and recommendation left online about them and the quality of their work from past companies and colleagues for whom they have worked on other temporary projects. It is up to the virtual worker to solicit, manage and update such references and recommendations and it is in their best interests to do so as their hire-ability and rate of pay will be determined by such online evidence.

The Trust Broker may have thousands of such workers, each with hundreds of recommendations, endorsements and comments (much like a less general LinkedIn or Yelp model) and will do the sorting of which workers would best suit a company's needs, presenting candidates with specific skills sets or experience to meet them.

The worker, in turn, will keep the Trust Broker aware of their availability, willingness to travel, any educational courses or training they add to their profile, changes in the type or length of projects they wish to pursue and any other updated information that would be of interest to a company wishing to hire them for a project.

The process on both sides begins when they Trust Broker and the virtual or temporary worker become aware of each other in the first place.

To better explain the idea how a Trust Broker works, let me introduce <u>People as a Service</u> as a case study.

We use social media extensively to communicate our existence and what we do to a broad range of skilled workers across the globe. Once we have been contacted or contact a prospective virtual worker, we do a full staffing process, speaking at length to each prospective virtual worker. We evaluate their skills, their facility with language, their work ethic, and how easy our dealings are with them. We do test project—either for us or a willing client for a low-profile project (one without a strict timeline or a high-risk). We hold their hands and evaluate, very carefully, how it goes.

When another customer then wants to do a very similar project, we already know the quality and capabilities of the freelancer we have worked previously and have a much better understanding of the quality he or she will be able to deliver for this new customer. With every additional project, the knowledge about the type of project, freelancer and potential outcome will improve and with this the quality of the whole system. Also, the more projects we do with them, the more the virtual worker wants to work with us. They get to stop beating the bushes for clients, worrying that the timeline is correct, that the project is well defined and that they will get paid.

It is not a perfect system, of course, since we are dealing with fallible humans on both sides of the equation. Success is a question of probability. If we work with the virtual freelancer 20 times, it is probable that the virtual worker will still be a good pick on the 21st use. The Trust Broker reduces risk. Here the real value of the trust broker becomes apparent. Without the trust broker, the knowledge gleaned from those projects and interactions would be, at best, limited to the freelancer. Company relationships and other customers would not benefit from that knowledge and the lessons would therefore largely be lost. With the trust broker model, the point is that the trust broker accumulates know-how about the type of project, the capabilities and approach to work of the freelancers and in combination of the two, achieves the perfect fit. Therefore, the company hiring a freelancer for the first time can take advantage of the full experience of the trust broker in finding the perfect fit for those types of projects, with that kind of customer, experience gained from past experiences with the freelancer the trust broker will propose. Such previous knowledge means the wheel need not be reinvented with each new project for which the company hires a freelancer, assuring better results for much lower transaction cost.

If life happens, a Trust Broker can accommodate changes in a virtual freelancer's circumstances (age, illness, willingness to accept fewer jobs). In order to do this, the Trust Broker has to have more than the 100 workers ready for use to accommodate 100 projects. We have to have a reserve of backup workers with similar skills and good reputation.

Companies will learn to take advantage of such dynamic and flexible virtual workers or may be left by the wayside by companies who do.

Every talent will be making "perfect "use of their talents and companies will only be investing capital and time into the "perfect" worker for their company. By integrating such a process, the growth potential will be enormous. Looking down the road about a decade, companies clinging to the old ways will see their growth slow and productivity fall off, so that the pressure will be so enormous that the companies learn and adapt. Thanks to this model, productivity will go through the roof and companies will be able to take advantage of many more opportunities than they have ever had before this change occurred.

Let's turn away for a moment to the 61% of employees' wasted time, their lack of productivity cited earlier in this book and their disengagement with the companies for which they work. By making use of Trust Brokers and virtual talent we see a solution to the productivity problem, the opportunity gap and we get an even clearer glimpse into the future of work:

- Efficiency is gained by not wasting that 61% of time/resources.
- Opportunities will be created if talent can be used properly. In the US alone, $500 billion can be saved from disengaged employees.
- Companies not taking advantage will be crowded out.

Such "crowding out" and sudden irrelevance has happened before. What happened to the horse population in the US when engines took over the transportation industry? There were 21 million horses reported in 1915. By 1957, their numbers were down to 750,000. Quite a drop from a "technology" so long considered irreplaceable.

The technology had radically changed. The horses weren't needed to plow or to pull the trolley car so they became obsolete almost overnight. The skilled labor known as "coopering", the industry of men who made barrels is another example. When is the last time you met a cooper? Yet companies remain blind to their own coming obsolescence until, often, it is too late. What symptom could they be harkening to now to avoid future obsolescence? Pain is symptom and often a motivator of change.

Companies are feeling pain at present due to the fact they are having a hard time finding the right talent they need to complete projects, create new products or services or make use of innovation. This is partially because they expect the worker to sit in their own office in whatever geographical location that is located. Virtual workers know no such shackles. They can work and live wherever they choose.

Companies feel pain when they find themselves failing to compete on the proper level; they need a new product; or they have a pool of employees that they need to do different work than they have been doing. This last one alone can cost a company millions of dollars and months of training.

Now, it is a given, that no company believes it is profitable enough, no matter who is doing the believing (the board of directors, the CEO or even his wife.)

Every company also believes it should be more innovative. For example, the Swiss watch industry invented both the wristwatch and automatic watch and was the leader for decades. They had an innovative idea yet again when they originated the digital watch, the Swiss didn't believe that the market would ever sift from the more traditional timepiece and the Japanese overtook the market completely.

This was much like what happened to Kodak. Once a market leader in film, Kodak understood itself as a paper and chemical company Kodak invited digital technology for use in cameras, but thought the technology had no future in the mass market. Blinded perhaps by their own heavy investment in paper and chemicals, Kodak lowballed the digital photo, went bankrupt in 2012 and had to emerge in 2013 as a much smaller company.

Profitability and innovation, as well as alleviation of these pain points, are possible through the use of the new work dynamic.

This new work model won't work everyone. Companies that are protected today, such as quasi-monopolies, entrenched bureaucracies or over-regulated industries, may find the required changes threatening or may not be able to take advantage of the opportunities.

On the talent side, the perfect marketplace won't work for everyone either. People who have a problem with technology won't be able to make the best use of this new dynamic. But many skilled workers may find their situation improved.

A restaurant dishwasher in New York won't be affected, but a knowledge worker sitting in an office in Manhattan, may find that though her current job has gone to a worker in Mumbai who has a great education, wonderful experience and will work for less. But the savvy New Yorker can now take the initiative, make her presence known to a Trust Broker and use her years of experience and great reputation to make more money, working when and where she wants and for as many projects and companies as she chooses.

Was it a good change that a lot of American manufacturing jobs went to China? Despite what populist American politicians say, I think it was a good thing because it is a win-win situation. The Chinese worker makes a huge increase in pay at a manufacturing plant as opposed to when they toiled in a field. A $500 iPhone for example, has $11 of manufacturing costs in it and another $200 in materials costs (that money goes to China), but the remaining profit remaining comes home to the USA. So the American company does in fact benefit in the end.

The market of the future will take some time to reach and some time for us to adjust to the differences it engenders, but it will, in time, become the way business is conducted. Big changes are ahead of us and they will be just as fundamental prior industrial revolutions. Not everyone will benefit, but most will. Later we will introduce different trust brokers for the market of work and explain how they are organized and the value they bring to the market.

Room will be made at the table for everyone and through increased efficiency, profit and talent availability, when the meal is served, there will be plenty on which to feast.

CHAPTER EIGHT

THE PERFECT MARKET FOR WORK: IMPLICATIONS FOR THE WORKFORCE AND SOCIETY AS A WHOLE

"L'avenir n'est plus aux positions mais aux trajectoires."

"The future is no longer in positions but trajectories."

–philosopher Michel Foucault

In the past, once a man had reached a certain high position in a company meant that had hit the pinnacle. He got the big mahogany desk, the corner office, the key to the Executive Washroom and he was allowed, to a certain extent, to rest on his laurels.

In the future market for work, that will no longer be so. The question will be asked of all, the highest and lowest paid employees of a company: What will you be able to achieve tomorrow? How much

204 | The Future of Work

influence can you yield to help the company, in its entirety, to succeed? Workers will no longer strive to become Senior VP, but will strive instead to give his or her best effort and make that effort count. The title will become unimportant. What will matter is what route your career has taken and what experiences and skills have you gathered along the way. Your trajectory is a combination of where you have been and where you want to go.

When we adjust our trajectory in that way and aim for a perfect market for work, what we once knew about work will fall away and, as a society, we will adjust our expectations and requirements of our workforce to the new paradigm.

Under the old system (and only after the abuses of the Industrial Revolution) labor laws were enacted, designed to protect workers. Such laws addressed the most egregious exploitation of workers (particularly children) who toiled in mills and factories serving capitalistic industrials who, unrestrained by any labor protections, almost to a man, exploited their workers. Unions came into being (not without a violent revolution of their own) and soon legislation was introduced, protecting workers, but extending such protections only those who held jobs at traditional companies.

Let's look at the political situation affecting labor laws in the United States:

Private sector rights protected under Federal and state law were created by the struggles and birthing pains of the labor movement. The eight-hour day was finally recognized by Congress in the Fair Labor Standards Act, (the "Wages and Hours Act"), of 1938, (though the struggle for the eight-hour day began at least as early as the 1880s, when the whole labor movement in the United States took part in political strikes on its behalf.)

Once the smoke had cleared, a list of rights recognized by Federal law included:

- The right to engage in concerted activity for mutual aid and protection (Section 7 of the National Labor Relations Act).
- The right not to be enjoined by Federal courts when engaging in such concerted activity (Section 4 of the Norris-LaGuardia Act).
- The right to refuse to perform abnormally dangerous work (Section 502 of the National Labor Relations Act, and the Occupational Safety and Health Act).
- The right to equal pay for equal work (the Equal Pay Act).
- The right to a minimum wage and to overtime pay after forty hours work in a week (the Fair Labor Standards Act).
- The right not to be discriminated against because of race, color, religion, sex, national origin, age, or disability in hiring, promotion, or discharge (Title VII of the Civil Rights Act and other laws).
- The right to free speech about union affairs, and to a minimum of due process when dis-

> ciplined by a union (Title I of the Labor Management Reporting and Disclosure Act).
> * The right to pension security (the Employee Retirement Income Security Act)[24]

Yet all of these rights laid the burden on the company who employed the workers at a time when more and more Americans were setting aside their plows and taking up industrial jobs. Within the span of a few decades from the late 19th to the early 20th century, the United States was transformed from a predominately rural agrarian society to an industrial economy centered in large metropolitan cities.

These changes were the direct result of the American Industrial Revolution that was founded on rising investment, employment, and productivity in the manufacturing sector. In 1880, when the agricultural frontier had largely disappeared, almost one-half of the American workers were still farmers and only one in seven workers (less than 15%) worked in manufacturing of any sort. But that would soon change thanks to the increasing urbanization of society and the shift of labor from farms to factories and offices. In 1880, workers in agriculture outnumbered industrial workers three to one, but by 1920, the numbers were approximately equal. Employment in the manufacturing sector expanded four-fold from 2.5 to 10 million

---

[24] *Where Do Workers' Rights Come From?* Retrieved February 10, 2016 from Industrial Workers of the World: http://www.iww.org/organize/laborlaw/Lynd/Lynd2.shtml

workers from 1880 to 1920.

Over the last decades, the market has shifted away from industrial jobs to mostly service jobs. Even within industrial companies, only a small portion of the employment is actually industrial in nature, with more positions within the company devoted to services such as R&D sales, purchasing and marketing.

We are undergoing another fundamental shift today. Now we see that even the very structure of employment is moving from a traditional employment concept to a freelancer and contractor concept. Look at some very successful companies of recent years and the number of traditional employees they have on their staffs: Airbnb, now the biggest hotel chain in the world, has only 1,600 employees (with a private valuation estimated at about $13 billion with rooms available in 34,000 cities in 190 countries—none of which Airbnb owns.)[25] or Uber, the largest taxi company in the world,[26] had "approximately 550 employees" in 2014, according to CEO, Travis Kalanick or Instagram that sold for billions to Facebook with only a handful of employees. Even more traditional com-

---

[25] Poletti, Therese. *What really keeps Airbnb's CEO up at night.* (2015, February 13). Retrieved December 12, 2015 from MarketWatch: http://www.marketwatch.com/story/what-really-keeps-airbnbs-ceo-up-at-night-2015-02-13

[26] Lagorio-Chafkin, Christine. *How Uber Is Going To Hire 1,000 People This Year.* (2014, January 15). Retrieved November 23, 2015 from Inc.com: http://www.inc.com/christine-lagorio/how-uber-hires.html

panies, like Apple, only directly employ a fraction of the people they need to get their products to market.

Labor laws created to be tied to traditional employment are no longer viable. If the goal of labor laws is protection of the weakest and to achieve a certain level of societal security, the tools from last century are not adequate anymore. Even worse, such antiquated legislation hinders innovation, and by protecting old industry ways, largely through legalistic tricks and well-worn work arounds, we are not only delaying necessary change, but actually hindering it. We can't stay rooted in the past and simultaneously stride forward into the future.

There is, of course, friction occurring as the old systems give way to the new. Class action suits are springing up all over the USA (and many European countries are forbidding the company from gaining a foothold at all) by persons who work as drivers for Uber. These drivers claim they are actually employees and should be paid and given benefits as such. Uber is also being sued for running an illegal business (for treating its drivers like contract workers while making them provide their own vehicles, insure them and maintain them. Since other taxi companies must operate under much more stringent conditions, they claim Uber is sliding under the radar by only employing "freelancers" and thus wiggling out of the responsibilities under which more traditional cab companies must operate.

AirBnB is another example. The company, which allows homeowners to rent out rooms in their homes by the night, isn't subject to the same safety inspection, health codes and tax structure under which traditional hotels must operate, thus posing unfair competition to hotels and motels of a more standard variety.

Companies like Uber and AirBnB seem to be getting away with murder and workers and owners who have been working for and running their businesses under the old model are angry. These examples show how labor laws that made perfect sense 100 years ago are getting in the way of new innovative approaches today. Such companies' growth has shown that they seem to offer better solutions for their customers than the legacy models do. That companies hide behind those laws in order to protect themselves from the new business models might slow progress, but will not be able to permanently delay change. This is similar in nature as what has started in the 1880's in the industrial labor movement.

This doesn't mean that we are going to do away with our entire legal system as it applies to the workforce and labor, only that the system must change if we are to avoid hindering innovation. Many of the same goals will be achieved, yet they will be approached in a different way.

Here is a discussion of some of those goals, how they have been handled in the past, and how we might achieve them in the future by adopting a new mindset:

Secure employment

Goal: To create full employment for all people of a working age.

Full employment should now be redefined as full occupation with necessary financial income achieved for all segments of the population who are of a working age.

Let begin by separating the two ideas—what differentiates a "job" and "work"? In the past, those two concepts were used as synonyms. A job was work for which you got paid. But that is not the proper definition of either word. Traditionally a "job" was something for which you got paid and "work" was where something got done.

As Scott Santens wrote in his article, "A Future Without Work Does Not Equal a Future Without Jobs.":[27]

> There is a huge difference between the two, and we must start seeing the difference, and making the difference clearer to each other. A job is what you are paid to do. It can either enable you to do work that you enjoy, or it can compensate you for doing work

[27] Santens, Scott. *A Future Without Jobs Does Not Equal a Future Without Work.* (2015, October 7). Retrieved October 27, 2015 from The Huffington Post: http://www.huffingtonpost.com/scott-santens/a-future-without-jobs-doe_b_8254836.html

that you do not at all enjoy. It can also even involve a whole lot of work or a complete lack of any work. The most important thing about a job is that we trade our time for monetary compensation.

Work is different… It's easier to see how money has nothing whatsoever to do with work. It's not part of the equation at all…Work can be necessary or entirely unnecessary. Work can be valuable or worthless. Work can be meaningful or empty. But all work is doing something instead of nothing, and no one can say the same thing about jobs.

*There are a lot of people out there getting paid to do absolutely **nothing**. There are also a lot of people out there getting paid nothing to do **everything**.*

…A new estimate put the amount of unpaid care work in the US economy as 5% of GDP, $691 billion, or 1.2 billion unpaid hours of work per week. Meanwhile, 2 million people spend 8.4 million hours every month in the US volunteering their time just for hunger relief.

…Consider this for a moment, and you may see work in an entirely new light. When you hate what you do as a job, you are definitely getting paid in return for doing it. But when you love what you do as a job or as unpaid work, you're only able to do it because of somehow earning sufficient income to enables you to do it.

Put another way, extrinsically motivated work is work done before or after an expected payment. It's an exchange. Intrinsically motivated work is work only made possible by sufficient access to money.

It's a gift.

The difference between these two forms of work cannot be overstated...

The future of work will also involve new forms of work that are very difficult for older generations to wrap their heads around as being work. ...We are experiencing an evolution of human work. We are entering a world of digital abundance where we find meaning in play and value in each other. Crossing the threshold of this world will require saying goodbye to old ways that cling to scarcity and an antiquated belief that jobs as we once knew them define us.

We are not defined by our jobs. We never have been. We are defined by our actions, and by the ways in which we seek meaning in our lives and with each other. And in this new world past the threshold, we'll finally begin to understand and appreciate the other side of creation - the enjoyment of what's created and the value in enjoying it.

Our immediate future involves recognizing old forms of work differently, new forms of work entirely, and the inherent value of simply enjoying our collectively created bounty together.

So we must set a goal for the new future of work. Is it to ensure everyone has a job and an income so that he/she can live and work or is our goal to ensure that every one can produce something of value?

Under the old the system, attempts were made to reach the goal of secure employment by making it hard for companies to fire employees, by taxing them to pay for people who lost their jobs, creating a big incentive to keep everyone they had hired employed.

In the perfect market for work, that scenario would not be the correct way to achieve the goal of allowing everyone to be able to produce something of value. If the object is not to keep everyone tied to the company (just to keep employment figures up), a company is free from having to maintain "deadwood" but also is able to make room for creative and motivated people to come work on projects for which they have a passion.

How can this be achieved without hindering business models of the future?

We need flexible work models, so connecting companies to benefits won't work anymore. The Social Security model and other legislation imposing such social benefits aren't the best tools to use in the future market, where our goal is to have nearly everyone employed at work they choose, when they choose it, not even hindered by age or geography. We need to set a goal of secure employment—employment that means everyone has a minimum income that allows him or her to live.

Many people contribute to the greater good of humanity by "working" without getting paid. A person who contributes their knowledge to update a Wikipedia page is contributing to us all, but is not getting paid for his effort. 100 million people, who work every day, don't get paid. They are stay-at-home mothers and no one would dispute their contribution to the world. We need to create a system wherein everyone receives the minimum income they need to maintain their life and health, while allowing then to do something valuable with their time.

In the old system, restrictions were put on employment contracts. Workers, except those with union protections or tenure, could be fired or given notice at any time. Workers, too, could decide on their own to leave for many reasons and had no protection once they had done so. Dependent on attaching themselves to a company for their wages and benefits, workers were at the mercy of employers' whims or the vagaries of the market.

In the new system, there will be a flexible market for work with market forces and fewer restrictions, assuring that most people have the work they need. Countries with low employment regulations, like Switzerland, Denmark and the United States, have relatively low unemployment, whereas countries with heavy regulation like France, Spain and Italy, have high unemployment. Left to such market forces, not only will the job market perform better (with lower structural unemployment) but companies will become more competitive, with higher growth.

Until the new market arrived, regulatory legislation limited companies' abilities to hire freelance and contract workers, instead forcing them into artificial strictures, such as the tax form 1099, where freelance workers are paid by the company as though they are employees, yet are given none of the benefits or provisions of true employees.

What will happen in the future is that a vast majority of workers can become their own boss, literally running their own one-man or one-woman company. Computer literacy will give everyone the tools to participate in the virtual market (no matter where in the world they are physically located).

Under the old system, educating employees was a task that fell to the employers who may have neglected formal training, forcing workers to learn on the job or trained employees inadequately or not at all, trapping workers in planned obsolescence.

The new market for work means there will be a new investment in education, which allows more students to become versed in the subjects they will need to compete in the new economy and such learning will no longer be dependent upon age, but will continue throughout one's lifetime. Job centers will become common, where counselors understand the virtual market for work and can steer workers towards new opportunities.

For those people who want to start their own companies, more support structures will arise geared towards helping individuals navigate the complexities of licensing, permitting and legalities necessary to launch their new venture. Capital will be freed up and stimulus packages ever more available for entrepreneurs and solopreneurs to help fund their businesses, Even commercial space sales and leasing will change, as modern working spaces will be built or converted to accommodate part-time, freelance and virtual workers.

Universal healthcare

Goal: To keep the population healthy and to provide for healthcare for all in times of need.

Under the old system, healthcare plans were company-sponsored based on plans negotiated by the company.

Today in the United States, healthcare is available for the majority of the population and should be affordable) and compulsory. The fly in the ointment, however, is that individuals, who find offerings hard to manage in the first place, have no negotiating power with insurance companies. Companies with many employees may "buy in bulk" as it were and are able negotiate much better deals for their employees. Also, if a company has a younger workforce that will compel an insurance company to offer better rates and, statistics also show that employed people are healthier than unemployed people, this also affects the rates the companies employees will be offered. Individuals will get less favorable rates and certainly those who are already sick will also only be offered higher rates.

The problem here is that not everyone will get the same insurance nor will everyone be operating on the same level playing field.

For the future of work, we must change to a system where insurance is compulsory ad affordable and where companies are out of the equation entirely. Such groups should concentrate on being employers and leave the insurance business to the individuals and their insurance companies to negation. The sick or weak or unemployed should have the same insurance available to tem as is available to everyone else.

Unemployment protection

Goal: To help families through times of temporary unemployment

Under the old system, there is a tax, on each worker's salary, paid by the company and the employee that comes off the top of each worker's paycheck in order to fund unemployment payments. The level of the salary at the worker's former job determines the amount of the payout and their eligibility for the benefits is based on the reason for the worker's joblessness. These payments are available for a limited amount of time and often may be extended, but only cover the bare minimum of an unemployed person's expenses. Since the unemployed person is teetering on the edge of financial disaster (which exacerbates stress, lowers self-esteem and can even break down physical health), the slide toward poverty and illness is swift. Once a person slides into poverty, say six months after he or she loses the job, it can be nigh onto impossible to get him/her out of it with *any* government help. Looking at the larger picture, where society has an investment in the success of every member, the investment made in the worker (through schooling, training, and allowing the person to gain invaluable job experience) is lost after about six months. The worker's value is diminished and their capabilities.

I propose, in the new market for work, that the government pay an unemployed worker's *reasonable* expenses (mortgage, school tuition, car payments, utilities, etc.) so that they do not lose their standard of living, for a delineated period of only 3-6 months, with no extensions available. Naturally, all that would be covered would be necessary expenses. If a worker had been making $10,000 per paycheck and needed only $5,000 to meet their expenses (with the rest going to savings), the government would only provide $5,000 in covered expenses. By having all the expenses covered, a worker can avoid the destructive downward spiral that leads to irreparable financial difficulties. The worker's value will be the same as it was before he or she lost his/her job and society wouldn't lose the investment made in the worker. Such a system will provide high incentive for the worker to get a new job quickly.

Social Security funding

Goal: To help the weakest of society escape poverty and live a dignified life.

As it stands, the Social Security program is funded by taxes paid by companies and employees via payroll deductions. Eligibility is based on income and family situation and payments are minimal, creating the horror stories of seniors living on cat food. Annual raises are not always annual and standard of living raises never keep pace with the increase in prices of food, housing or other basic necessities.

For all that the United States is one of the richest countries in the world, the social net it provides many parts of society doesn't reflect its prosperity. Whereas it might be argued that European countries protections are too strong, the United States' protections are too weak. We must strike a balance, but we can no longer ignore the fact that the less well we take care of our social ills (our elderly and disables, the 30% of adult black males who have or will have been incarcerated in prisons, the rising tide of teenage pregnancies, those for whom food stamps means only avoidance of starvation), the more societal tensions and unrest rises.

In the new future of work, we must rethink social security funding. It should no longer be based on employment, but be a government expense allocating funding to be distributed to help cover those social ills that affect us all of society. Poverty creates problems and we must rebuild a system that allows us to protect our most vulnerable, our elderly and disabled, from falling into its black hole. We must pay stricter attention to the concept of "social" in social security. It is a moral imperative.

Care for these people should also be provided and these positions might be filled by workers who don't "have a job", but rather provide their valuable services as part of work in the purest sense. Their contributions, like a stay-at-home parent's, provide a value service to us all.

Trade Unions

Goal: To protect the weakest members of the formal workforce from the capitalistic companies hoping to maximize profits by acting against the interest of the labor force.

The old system dictated that a relatively uneducated work force needed to gain some power in their essentially powerless situation. Labor unions, for a dues-paid membership and an agreement to act in concert with the goals of the union, provided education on the issues and strength in numbers (resulting in collective bargaining) making use of spokesman to represent the workers, stating their case and instituting work stoppage as the most effective tool in the workers' "arsenal".

In the perfect market for work, the power does not lie with the company anymore, but with all participants in the market (both companies and talent). Individual relationships will be stressed. Labor unions will be replaced with interest groups at all levels to protect the different members to the market and formulate regulation where they benefit the market as a whole. Labor disputes like strikes and work stoppages will be prohibited. Further legislation will only be concocted as a last resort and only when a thorough mediation process has failed and the political process was unable to resolve the issues.

Discrimination

Goal: No one shall be discriminated against because of age, religion, race, gender, disability or sexual orientation.

The old method tried to solve the problem through rule of law. Legal proceedings were the recourse to impose those laws when someone felt he or she had been a victim of discrimination. Companies were barred from asking certain questions (the applicant's age, marital status, childbearing plans, race, sexual preferences) during job interviews in order to use the information to influence the company's hiring decision.

However with today's information, both private and professional, being readily available to nearly everyone through social media, the issue of proprietary personal information and the specter of discrimination is one not so easily dismissed. In the future of work certain factors about which an applicant might face discrimination will become moot. A person's age or marital status are irrelevant as people become virtual workers able to work well past classic "retirement age" and no longer hindered by, for example, having to relocate when his or her spouse does. In the age of the internet, the "have laptop will travel" culture will eliminate many of the former reasons for possible discrimination, but new ways to prevent discrimination from hindering minority and other vulnerable workers will have to be implemented to protect those workers most at risk.

I understand that change is scary—it always has been and not doubt such fear will last as long as the human condition. But change is necessary to improve the market of work for all.

Some fearmongers run through social discourse as though their hair was on fire, yelling that the sky is in fact falling and we will all soon be replaced by machines.

It is true that Uber's CEO has publically stated that he fully intends to replace all Uber's part-time drivers with automated cars at the earliest opportunity.

But barring Uber, it is unlikely human workers are about to be replaced by a robot.

As is pointed out in an article published in *The Economist*[28], we've been dealing with such fears since the Industrial Revolution, when handloom weavers were so resistant to the new-fangled machines that they earned a new name, "Luddites", that sticks with us up to the present day as a byword for anyone trying to stop technological progress. Such anxiety hasn't left us. Many of us fear that a "bucket of bolts" (or drives and circuits) will take our jobs.

David Autor[29], an economist at MIT quoted in the article, points out that those with a gloomy view of automation are disregarding the many jobs that come into being thanks to the very existence of whizz-bang new machines. Only that, he argues, can explain why the share of America's population in work rose during the 20th century despite dazzling technological advances, or why the drop in agricultural employment, from 40% of the workforce to 2%, did not lead to mass unemployment. The new jobs that technology makes possible, Autor argues, more than compensate for

[28] *Automation Angst.* (2015, August 15). Retrieved September 23, 2016 from The Economist: http://www.economist.com/node/21661017

[29] Autor, David H. 2015. "Why Are There Still So Many Jobs? The History and Future of Workplace Automation." *Journal of Economic Perspectives*, 29(3): 3-30. Retrieved September 23, 2016 from the American Economic Association: https://www.aeaweb.org/articles.php?doi=10.1257/jep.29.3.3

those lost through substitution. It is just easier to identify the disappearing, but familiar occupations, than it is to foresee the new ones created in their stead.

Also, the author counsels, one way to think about the impact of technology is by categorizing the tasks involved in any job between cognitive and manual on the one hand, and routine and non-routine on the other hand. It is occupations in administration and middle management, which involve cognitive but routine tasks, which have been the most vulnerable to automation so far. By contrast, employees whose work is cognitive but not routine have largely gained from technological change, since it enables them to process and present information more readily. Likewise, many forms of manual employment have proved difficult to computerize, and have thus been largely unaffected.

This explains a pattern that has become common in the labor markets of advanced economies in recent decades, whereby there has been growth in employment at both the top and the bottom of the spectrum, but a hollowing-out in the middle.

Such comforting resilience may not last as machine begin to take on both previously manual jobs (thanks to advances in automation) and non-routine ones (courtesy of improvements in artificial intelligence). We harken back to the Uber example, with its soon-to-be robotic drivers. Robotics expert, Gill Pratt writes, "If this potential were to be realized, robots could march off the production lines where they carry out specific tasks and take over a far more diverse set of roles in large parts of the economy, including manual occupations. One much touted example would be driverless vehicles, which could endanger the livelihoods of legions of taxi drivers and couriers."

But before you panic for all your checkered cab cohorts, Autor further argues that many jobs still require a mixture of skills, flexibility and judgment; they draw upon "tacit" knowledge that is a very long way from being codified or performed by robots. Moreover, automation is likely to be circumscribed, he argues, as politicians fret about wider social consequences. Most important of all, even if they do destroy as many jobs as pessimists imagine, many other as yet unimagined ones that cannot be done by robots are likely to be created.

In 1930, John Maynard Keynes published a famous essay that predicted that the grandchildren of his generation would scarcely have to work at all. Keynes regarded that as a sign of progress, whereas many today fear such an outcome. *The Economist* article concludes, "Current predictions of the obliteration of jobs may be as far off the mark as Keynes' hopelessly rosy view."

So apparently we are all not going to be replaced by automation, but what are the some of the societal repercussions that may occur courtesy of the upcoming perfect market for work?

As a start, the whole organizing principles—of

capital and work were built around the model of traditional employer/employee— is going the way of the Model T.

Much of what is called "the nanny state" will fade away for those able to work. Labor laws and legislation will adjust to make way for a new generation of workers unlike any seen in the history of labor.

As their own boss, workers will be responsible for furthering their education and mastering skills needed to compete in a virtual global pool of talent. A college degree or even an advanced degree will no longer guarantee a good position.

Workers will have to initiate contacts, nurture relationships and be resourceful. They must make getting and keeping a reputation as a useful, reliable and skilled worker an ongoing priority.

Workers will be exposed to and absorb technical knowledge easily. It will no longer count as specialized knowledge but will be organic in society.

People must take care of their health and take it upon themselves to secure health insurance and the medical care they need.

We, as a civilized nations, must take care of the old, the sick and those unable to work, though the definition of "unable to work" will take on new meaning when even handicapped people, or those that are geographically isolated, will be able to take on jobs in the new market for work.

Parents will arrange their own "parental leave" and will make childcare arrangements by accepting or rejecting freelance or virtual projects on their own schedule.

Individuals will set their own pay—charging whatever they find the market will bear based on their experience and reputation. Men will no longer be paid more than women unless women themselves set their pay lower than the males with whom they compete for jobs.

Social Security and other government programs instituted as a safety net will still exist, but will be funded differently and workers can choose to opt out of the system to handle investing for their retirement privately.

Borders will disappear. If a worker qualifies for a job in another country, he or she can accept that job and work remotely, competing in skills (and cost) with workers from all over the world.

Finally we will get to the age were we will all work and not just have a job. Not all work will make money, but all of it will create value and add to our store of knowledge with the added benefit of helping to create a good reputation for the person who shared. For example, those who share what they know on a computer forum or those who debate the meaning of medieval manuscripts in a user group, are all showing off their expertise (which enhances reputation, perhaps leading to a future consultancy) and creating value for the rest of us.

Most importantly, in the perfect market, all who want to work will work, in a position that interests them, on projects that make the most of their skills and talents, and for a fair rate of pay they set themselves.

Perfect Market for Work and its Impact on Society as a Whole

As I discussed above when I delineated the difference between work and a job, in the perfect market for work we will see more people will work and less people will have jobs. Some of that work will be paid and other work will not be paid directly, but will offer other compensation—a feeling of worth, happiness at having contributed to the greater good, perhaps even satisfaction at having advanced the human race. New creative models of income generation will have to be developed to insure those individuals that generate work, but do not receive direct pay for that work, are able to have an income sufficient to meet their needs.

Some things to ponder:

- Work well done creates a good reputation, which, in turn, creates work that gets paid, likely at a higher level than had been paid before when the worker may not have been as skilled or experienced at the task.
- Certain types of work will generate profitable intellectual property rights, such as articles, white papers, video presentations, web content and graphics that will continue to create future profit.

- Work that generates interest (followers, fans, clicks) for a blog, website or video project generates income through allowing advertisers to hawk their wares on the site where such work is featured. Interest is created when the work is of high enough quality to catch the eye of followers and fans and, through them, potential advertisers.
- Work that is valuable to a contingency will be paid through donations by that contingency. Campaigns like Kickstarter and Crowdfunding already make use of campaigns to garner support. Like-minded people are exposed to a campaign to support a project, movement, product (or the person behind such ideas) and then express their support by putting money towards the idea to allow it to continue to unfold.
- More start-ups and entrepreneurs will rise to the level of awareness in the new model of work. If they create value and reach a certain level of success, their business models will attract investors. If they exceed even that success, they will create spinoffs. In the event of success, the rewards are much higher than regular paid work, but it must be noted that the risk of achieving no financial reward is much higher as well.
- Work is sometimes undertaken for a greater good, which brings personal satisfaction and recognition by society and peer groups.

As Maslow described in his "Hierarchy of Needs," once a person's basic needs for food, shelter and safety are met, non-monetary rewards become more important. He eventually progresses to the level of self-actualization that can be described as "What a man can be, he must be". The future of work will allow people to work in areas that fulfill the higher levels of Maslow's pyramid, bringing them much more satisfaction than a mere job ever could.

- Work creates learning. Work can create knowledge and precipitate connections that will allow for new types of work in the future, for which workers will be better compensated, as they now know more than they knew before the change.

These are, of course, only some of the new concepts of work, which will spring up. We can, from where we stand, always only see through a glass darkly. It would have been impossible to imagine only a few years ago that a young man from Sweden, who calls himself PewDiePie and plays expletive-laden video games and then posts the videos online, would earn $12 million from advertisers who want to be seen on his site[30]. I'm sure there will be many more substantial projects and pieces

[30] *The World's Highest-Paid YouTube Stars 2015.* (2015, October 14). Retrieved January 12, 2016 from Forbes.com: http://www.forbes.com/sites/maddieberg/2015/10/14/the-worlds-highest-paid-youtube-stars-2015/

of work which will add to our knowledge as a race once we are fully freed from the chains of geography, age, previous experience and the "way it's always been done." We will see strides in medicine and science, the arts, mathematics and solutions to problems like feeding the hungry and caring for our elderly will emerge.

Winners and Losers in the Perfect Market for Work

Even though the perfect market for work will present opportunities for most people, some people will always see the trees rather than the forest, the problems rather than the opportunities. Some people will be unable to adapt and, just as in nature, without growth, the tree withers. Here are some of the people who will be negatively affected in the upcoming perfect market for work:

Lower qualified knowledge workers in high-income countries will lose because:

- There will be lots of new competition.
- Knowledge work, such as theirs, can be done virtually.
- Workers with similar or even better skills from lower income countries will become competitors and the lower price they charge will serve as a power incentive to hire them.

Workers with a low level of energy and motivation will be beat out because:

- The perfect market for work will convert

many workers into entrepreneurs who will promote themselves as well as their business.

- Results are what will count in the new market and simply showing up for work and doing the minimum to keep one's job won't be accepted.

People with no access to communication technology will be bypassed because:

- Such access will be vital, specifically for knowledge workers trying to market themselves as a virtual asset.
- Onsite workers will need access to their computers 24/7 as jobs will no longer be a 9-5 proposition.

People with high resistance to change will fall by the wayside because:

- Ready or not, the changes to the markets for work are going to change and workers can either get on the bandwagon or get out of the way. The juggernaut will roll.
- Resisting or rejecting the coming changes will use up all the time and energy a worker has to give, rendering them unsuitable for the new market.

People in a job who really don't do much work and like it that way will be upset because:

- The likelihood that the employer will change the way the project gets done and he/she needs movers and shakers to help push the product or solution through to completion means the person who doesn't do much work will be considered an impediment to efficiency.

- Such a worker will generate neither results nor any value. This renders the worker him or herself as of little value.
- Having gotten used to working hours as opposed to generating results will mean the worker is soon off the project, replaced by someone who truly does work.

People with poor working attitude will need to adjust their attitude in the new market for work or find themselves without work because:

- Should they be hard to work with, their reputation will precede them and they will get fewer offers.
- Teams will not choose them as an additional team member, even on a temporary project, denying them not only the ability to add information to the group, but disallowing them from adding to their own story of knowledge and expertise.
- After starting out with a poor attitude and exacerbated by the fact that employers, teams and other individuals don't want to help or share with them, this intractable employee's results will be mediocre, meaning he will get less offers in the future.

The perfect market for work will also affect people in physical jobs that cannot be outsourced to virtual workers. As we have examined previously, when we were discussing how construction companies would adapt to the new market, seeing as how most of their workers must be onsite and there is not room for shoddy work, the requirements may change less than in jobs which can become largely virtual. What is required are physical presence and a flexible work market wherein results will count even more so than in the past. These types of jobs do have some advantages to them:

- Due to the nature of such jobs, competing talent need to be local with similar cost structures.
- Most physical jobs will not find themselves in in competition with machines. Some knowledge workers will have to yield their jobs because automated systems really can do a better job that a human, but this is not totality of such jobs. Machines may help, but not replace humans when it comes to building a house, waiting tables in a restaurant or caring for the sick.

Some talent is specifically well positioned to benefit from the perfect market for work and will adapt easily in the early stages. Such workers will be found among those:

- Highly qualified for virtual work
- Possessed of a good social reputation and a strong network to recommend them.
- Those workers who are adept at doing real work and not satisfied with only having a

job.
- Those workers with a highly specialized talent.
- Technology savvy workers in areas where technology is a key accelerator
- Young entrepreneurs who come up with innovative ideas and problem solving notions for a fraction of the cost as previous concepts and solutions.
- Middle to highly qualified knowledge workers hailing from low-income countries who speak good English.

Human vs. Machine

From *The Matrix* to the *Terminator* movies, popular culture has played upon our innate fear that in the inevitable war of man vs. machine, machines are bound to win. When robots took over much of the manufacturing in Detroit automaker's factories, when automating replaced many humans in customer service jobs, right up to today's rumor that Uber is working its way to replacing all of its drivers with robot drivers, we are concerned that this is one evolutionary race in which we humans won't come out on top.

Non-technical people aren't the only ones concerned. Some of the tech world's most prominent visionaries have weighed in on the issue and some have taken some surprising positions. Microsoft founder, Bill Gates, shared concerns about the threat artificial intelligence will pose to humanity, and theoretical physicist Stephen Hawking, (who relies heavily on machine learning and artificial intelligence to communicate, argued such artificial intelligence could spell the end of the human race. Tesla Motors CEO Elon Musk even likened AI to "summoning a demon."[31]

The author of the article from which the above quotes are taken, former Chief Architect for Lockheed Martin's Visual World Labs Richard Boyd, studied the relationship between humans and machines for many years. He came to believe that the central issue of the 21st century is not machines taking over; it's how to achieve the right balance between humans and automation to optimize outcomes.

The most valuable resource we have in the universe is intelligence, which is simply information and computation; however, in order to be effective, technological intelligence has to be communicated in a way that helps humans take advantage of the knowledge gained. The optimal way to solve this problem is a combination of human and machine intelligence working together to solve the problems that matter most—from driverless cars to prevents millions of accidents, to robot guided

[31] Boyd, Richard. *Man Vs. Machine: How Humans Are Driving The Next Age of Machine Learning*. (2015, June 11). Retrieved January 13, 2016 from techcrunch.com: http://techcrunch.com/2015/06/11/man-vs-machine-how-humans-are-driving-the-next-age-of-machine-learning/#.hlb1wg:gSSP

surgery to micromappers to speed up relief on the scene of the world's devastating natural disasters.

As I have pointed out above, intelligence, artificial or otherwise, is to be utilized, harnessed and appreciated for the benefits it can and will bring to mankind. We should not be worried about competition but rather concentrate on cohesion.

We should be looking at the equation as humans plus machines, not humans or machines.

Dr. John Kelly, senior vice president of IBM Research, at the Augmenting Human Intelligence Cognitive Colloquium, contended that artificial intelligence can augment human intelligence — by helping us make sense of the quintillion bytes of data generated each day.

It's not about machines gaining intelligence or taking over the world, said Kelly. It's not even about recreating the human brain or its basic architecture. It's about taking inspiration from the brain — or whatever inspiration from wherever we can get it — and changing the current computing architecture to better handle data and further our understanding of the world.

Around 80% of data is unstructured; meaning that current computing systems can't make sense of it. By 2020, this number will reach 93%. Kelly, and other leaders in the field, believe there are valuable nuggets hidden amongst all that data and believe artificial intelligence will help uncover those nuggets.

We don't yet, for example have a way to analyze the millions of gigabytes of health related data generated by a person over the course of their lifespan, yet such information, properly parsed could hold the key to curing disease or adding to our information in order to better manage care. We are limited by our own human capability and that marvel of technology, made by our hand — the silicon chip.

But we aren't limited for long. IBM and Cornell University have developed a chip named True North, which works like our mammalian brain.

TrueNorth mimics the brain by wiring 5.4 billion transistors into 1 million "neurons" that connect to each other via 256 million "synapses." The chip doesn't yet have the ability to incorporate dynamic changes in synaptic strength, but the team is working towards it and, with such work, we are "trying to augment human intelligence with AI, not replicate it," say the developers of the chip.

It's a great example of human and machine synergy. Human intuition drives machines forward, and machines in turn augment human intelligence with interpretable data.

"We're building sophisticated, autonomous and intelligent systems that are extensions and collaborators of ourselves," says Dr. Myron Diftler, a scientist that constructs robots at the NASA Johnson Space Center in a panel discussion. "It's a humans plus machines future."[32]

So we see that the future of work will not be dominated by either human or machine, but a combination of the two, resulting in a symbiotic relationship where both partners serve the other, both becoming stronger and better for the fact that they act in tandem, each playing off the strengths of the other.

Let's look at how this human/machine collaboration could benefit one of our society's repetitive (and most important) tasks. In a traditional school system, a teacher repeats the same math lesson in the same way to her class of 35 students, on an annual basis, year after year, sharing the same knowledge, in the same way. Over a single year, teachers all over the world may have shared that same lesson thousands of times with their classes. Were the teacher to make use of a machine to impart the lesson to her students, she could utilize the time which has been freed up from her schedule to actually teach her students—answering their questions, going over their work, encouraging them to do better, understanding when a roadblock is an issue—in all ways, being more helpful to other students. The teacher can make use of a vast pool of available materials (such as is available from Kahn Academy) and the students can make use of

[32]   Fan, Shelly. *Forget Humans Vs. Machines: It's a Humans + Machines Future*. (2015, October 14). Retrieved January 14, 2016 from SingularityHUB: http://singularityhub.com/2015/10/14/forget-humans-vs-machines-its-a-humans-machines-future/

technology in a way that best speaks to them (the written word, audio, visual, or perhaps concepts presented in graphics or even video games.) With the human teacher as a guide and that educator having more free time thanks to the collaboration with a machine, the student and the educational system both benefit.

The healthcare system will also be able to make great use of a partnership between man and machine. Not only can machines run tests, analyze symptoms and make suggestions of pre-diagnoses, thus freeing up time for both nurses and doctors, but can integrate not only a patient's medical history, but that of their family, identifying a family history and, with that, eliminating much of the guesswork for the diagnostician. Wearable technology will also be able to do constant monitoring of certain indicators of health, giving results that today's once-every-year check-up can never match. It is estimated that 95% of heart attack-related death could be avoided had the symptoms of a heart attack been recognized earlier. By integrating and interpreting the medical history of thousands of people worldwide. New patterns of disease may become apparent and a cure that more quickly found once such analyzed data is available.

An analyst will be instantly able to dissect worldwide financial trends. An entertainer can dig up timely material to entertain his audience all with the tap of a key. We will be able to monitor, analyze and understand in the timeliest of ways how climate change in the farthest reaches of the globe will and are affecting us where ever we are.

As Erik Brynjolfsson and Andrew McAfee point out their book, *The Second Machine Age*,[33] the new abundance of data, data points and information coupled with the capability to use all that wealth of information in a sensible way, will allow us to be able to work together with the machines to create something much more powerful in the future than we have ever had in the past.

The future of work is a bright one. By pursuing sound policies which allow for new ideas to flourish and new business models to compete with the old ones without distortion, we will be able to move into a future of work that will bring value to society and more satisfying work for most people without having to endure the negative impacts that revolutionary change might bring with it. It will be vital for everyone involved in such change, the politicians, business owners and workers, to embrace such change letting go of tensions and conflicts. The future of work must flow free and unfettered and will therefore be able to quench everyone's thirst.

---

[33] Brynjolfsson, Erick and Andrew McAfee (2015). *The Second Machine Age: Work, Progress, and Prosperity in a Time of Brilliant Technologies*. New York: W.W. Norton & Company January 25, 2016.

CHAPTER NINE

TRUSTBROKERSINTHENEW MARKET FOR WORK

"It is mutual trust, even more than mutual interest,
that holds human associations together."

—*H. L. Mencken, journalist and cultural critic.*

Introduction

As we have seen in previous chapters the market for work is broken.

Companies lose billions of dollars every year due to disengaged employees or missing talent; while at the same time, talented workers are trapped in jobs that do not motivate them. In the United States alone, this is estimated to cost about $500 billion every year.

In order to fix the market for work, five elements are needed to allow this transformation to happen and some are already in place:

- Technology to facilitate remote work — Element in place

- Cheap, universal communication and internet access —Element in place
- Organizational concepts that divide jobs into portions that can be done remotely — This division is underway and becoming more common.
- Culture to work together in new ways—The new generation of workers is becoming familiar with such a concept
- Transparent and efficient market to bring talent and jobs together—This is being accomplished by the introduction of Trust Brokers.

What is a Trust Broker?

Imagine a situation where every company knew about every virtual freelancer on the planet and had an understanding of that freelancer's availability, price for service, experience, capabilities, weaknesses and reliability. Such knowledge would allow a company to always find the perfect freelancer for every remote job position. Now imagine the freelancers could discover and analyze all the available remote jobs. What was the timeline and deadlines for the proposed job? How much did it pay? What experience, education or capability was required? What was the company like to work for and did they pay on time and fully? The freelancer could assume, with this information, whether he or she might fit the job proposed and would enjoy working on the project if an employment agreement were reached.

Such comprehensive information is out of the reach of both the company looking to hire a freelancer and the freelancer looking for remote projects on which to work. On both sides of the equation, the effort to learn and understand the whole market would require such time and effort that the costs to gain such knowledge would significantly outweigh the benefits.

What is needed is a middleman, a broker trusted by both sides, who knows not only what jobs are available at the companies, but also the freelancers that comprise the global talent pool who might be perfectly qualified to fill those available jobs. The business owner would not need to find and then establish and maintain relationships with many virtual freelancers, he or she need only establish and maintain a relationship with one trust(ed) broker who understands the company's needs and could help fill available positions as they arose from a pool of virtual freelancers with whom the trust broker has worked previously. Conversely, instead of having to take time and effort to market themselves to companies searching for their very skills, a freelancer need only know the trust broker who would act in the freelancer's stead as a sales and marketing agent. The "product" the trust broker would represent would be the freelancer him/herself.

In the last years many platforms have evolved

to help customers tap into the global pool of virtual freelancers. Those platforms can be divided into two main categories:

- Self-service platforms
- Full-service proposal platforms

Self-service platforms share similar traits. They are:

- Transaction-based (Limited to a one-time transaction relationship between the customer, the platform and the freelancer).
- Consumer-focused: Even though many projects are for businesses, the concept is consumer-oriented. Projects are simple, one-time projects with low strategic value and are being outsourced to the platform for opportunistic reasons.
- No support by the platform: the customer gets only limited support for the description of the project, the selection of the right person and the support during the delivery of the project. The platform does provide a long list of potential candidates, but the candidates are not vetted and the only support a customer gets are the ratings from past customers and these are of limited value. As an example, nearly 90% of rated freelancers on the leading self-service platform Upwork are rated between 4 and 5 stars out of 5
- Knowledge is not captured: Every project that is being done creates a body of knowledge about the project description, the selec-

tion, the customer and the freelancer who is working on the project. Since most customers do not repeat same or similar projects, the knowledge gained from each experience is mainly lost. The only references to past projects are the less-than-helpful customer ratings.

There are two types of Self-Service Platforms: Vertical Platforms and General Platforms.

Vertical platforms focus on a certain capability like Design, Writing, Legal or other specific vertical markets, while General Platforms are free-for-all marketplace, offer workers with all levels of experience in all types of businesses. Online marketplaces often manage the payments and make money by charging membership fees and/or "marking up" on the billings of the contractors/freelancers. The mark-ups can range from 5 percent to 15 percent.

Here are some examples of General Platform companies:

Upwork (formerly Elance/oDesk)

Elance was initially developed as a technology for supporting virtual work. In 2006 Elance developed its current web-based platform for online, contingent work.

oDesk created an online workplace to allow distributed teams to work together and help instill trust in work happening via the Internet. oDesk has freelancers available to do any type of remote work, with no vertical market specialty. The company uses a type of talent exchange where contingent workers, contractors and freelancers can offer their skills and services for limited projects or even on-going assignments and where organizations and individuals can post their requirements or put tasks/projects out to bid.

For its clients, the Upwork/Elance website allows businesses to post jobs, search for freelance professionals, and solicit proposals. They can evaluate the contractors applying for the job and, once a contractor is selected, communications and files are exchanged through the Elance system. Payment for jobs, which can either be hourly-rate or project-based jobs, is made by the client through Elance's system, which deducts a percentage of the fee, 8.75%, as a "commission." Elance offers a Work View tool provides an official record of work completed. For project-based jobs statement of work or milestones are used to indicate progress toward completion, and funds are held in escrow by Elance to ensure payment upon completion of the milestone.

Freelancers using the Elance website may search for jobs and can research clients' buying histories on the system. Each freelancer can post a profile displaying past jobs and feedback, a portfolio, and specific skill and educational-background information. Registered free users are allowed to submit a limited number of proposals each month while those on paid membership plans can submit additional proposals. Elance offers payment guarantee once work is done using the Elance system.

Freelancer.com

Freelancer is a global outsourcing marketplace, which allows potential employers to post jobs that freelancers can then bid to complete. The site allows employers to post work to get done. Anybody is then able to offer quotes to complete the project, upon which point the original employer is able to award the work. Freelancer has different levels of membership. Free accounts can only bid on 8 projects per month and cannot make direct deposit withdrawals. Higher tiers of paid accounts get additional bids, direct deposit withdrawals, and other features.

Freelancer takes a 10% fee from all projects for most levels of membership, with a minimum fee of $5. Freelancer uses a "rewards" system where freelancers earn XP for performing actions such as "Like us on Facebook", by earning XP the user can "level up" his or her account and unlock rewards, including basic features such as being able to bid more times per month. However, only paid accounts actually get the benefits of these rewards.

Fiverr

Fiverr is a global online marketplace offering tasks and services, beginning at a cost of $5 per job performed, from which it gets its name. The site is primarily used by freelancers, who use Fiverr to offer services to customers worldwide. Currently, Fiverr lists more than three million services on the site that range between $5 and $500. Recently, however, the company lifted that limit with a new tier system, in a bid to allow freelancers worldwide to use Fiverr as their main venue for reaching clients. The site is used primarily by young people. Only two percent of the sellers are over the age of 55. Services (called "gigs") are offered in various areas from designing a business card to allowing buyers to purchase the services of a puppet to make a birthday video.

PeoplePerHour

PeoplePerHour is a UK-based company that provides a website for the advertisement of freelance work, largely in design, marketing, writing and software development. The majority of clients using the services are small companies that do not want to hire a full-time professional. This type of online marketplace is referred to as "crowdsourcing" – using a virtual network to outsource work. Clients may browse Hourlies™: fixed price offers ready to start immediately (with a minimum of a job which takes only an hour to complete), post a job to let freelancers find them or search profiles of freelancers and contact them directly. A down payment is paid and final payment can be made through the site at the end of the project. Testimonials are posted by both the clients and the freelancers about the project on which they worked. Projects include such things as adding 150 "likes" to a company's YouTube account for $10 to "writing any message on my finger and sexily biting it in a photo" for $13.

Guru.com

Guru.com is a freelance marketplace, allowing companies to find freelance workers for commissioned work and as an online clearinghouse for high tech workers seeking short-term contracts. Guru.com uses the Internet to provide new kinds of services where individuals negotiate directly with potential employers. Guru developed the SmartMatch technology that matches résumés and other information about job applicants to jobs. It also developed a candidate profiling system, using techniques from industrial and organizational psychology to better understand a candidate's suitability for a particular job. Guru's technology and staff focus on software to help large employers assess and hire job applicants.

Vertical Self-Service Platforms:
99Designs

99designs is an online graphic design marketplace. The company creates their products by crowdsourcing, as customers can solicit designers to submit designs for contests to create products such as websites, t-shirts, or logos. The customer then chooses the best design from the pool of submitted entries and the selected designer will win a cash payment. All other designers, whose designs were not selected, receive no compensation. Customers also have the option of working with individual designers by purchasing design templates from 99designs' Readymade logo store or by visiting Swiftly for quick graphic design fixes and logos.

DesignCrowd

DesignCrowd is an online crowdsourcing site with graphic designers signed up from 165 countries who outsource or crowdsource logo, website, print and digital design to businesses around the world. The client posts a "contest" describing their project, posts a budget and waits for designers to send designs. The client either asks for changes or gives other feedback, waits for responses, picks a winner and the designer gets paid after sending competed files (and signing off on the copyright for the design.) All designers who submitted designs for the contest are not compensated for their design unless it is the one that was selected.

Amazon Mechanical Turk

Amazon Mechanical Turk is a crowdsourcing internet marketplace that enables individuals and businesses (known as "Requesters") to coordinate the use of human intelligence to perform tasks that computers are currently unable to do. Employers are able to post jobs known as HITs (Human Intelligence Tasks), such as choosing the best among several photographs of a storefront, writing product descriptions, or identifying performers on music CDs. Workers (called "Providers" in Mechanical Turk's Terms of Service, or, more colloquially, "Turker"s) can then browse existing jobs, parceled out by the company one job at a time and complete them for a monetary payment set by the employer. To place jobs, the requesting programs uses an open application programming interface (API) or the more limited MTurk Requester site. Projects posted generally pay from .01 cent to $25 to the Provider. Mechanical Turk was started by Amazon for themselves in order to have humans look at similar product descriptions, pictures or products and decided whether they are the same or not. Computers are not able to fulfill that task accurately. This model was so successful that Amazon decided to open it up to all.

HourlyNerd

HourlyNerd4 is a global online marketplace that connects companies of all sizes with over 10,000 independent business consultants for project-based work. The HourlyNerd platform enables clients to post projects, receive bids (usually between 475 and

$200 per hour), interview and select experts, track projects, and make payment on the site. Typical project types include strategic advisory, marketing and branding, finance, and operations. There are more than 10,000 independent consultants on the HourlyNerd platform. 90% of these "Nerds" have MBAs from top 40 global programs, and they have an average of 8+ years of work experience. A project fee is collected when the buyer selects a consultant, but the money is held until the project is complete, and don't pay your nerd until we know you're fully satisfied. For recurring part-time work (with an individual or group of MBA consultants), weekly or bi-weekly payment agreements may be arranged. For placement of full-time hires, the site charges 18% of the first year's salary. This option comes with a 3-month guarantee, whereby the fee paid to HourlyNerd will be refunded in full if the long-term hire leaves the hiring firm, for any reason, during the guarantee period. The company is working to develop a recruiting platform and HourlyNerd's enterprise software solution is currently in private beta mode.

Toptal

Toptal is a global network of freelance software developers and designers that claims, after a rigorous screening process, to only hire the top 3% of freelancers in their specialties. Toptal provides companies with designers, engineers, and teams on an hourly, part-time, or full-time basis for any web, mobile, or desktop technology stack or design environment. Clients detail their needs and Toptal staff matches the needs with a software developer or designer who fits the requirement. If, within two weeks, of starting the project, a client is dissatisfied, the project is free and a client may choose up to 5 Toptal freelancers to assure a cultural fit. An average cost for a designer on Toptal is $1,800 - $3,200+/week for a full-time Front-End or Back-End Engineer. A $500 deposit is required and applied to the first invoice. Toptal takes a commission off the fee the client pays.

Project4Hire

Project4Hire is a freelance marketplace that connects hiring clients to freelance professionals and contractors all over the world. Clients post jobs or their project scope, along with their requirements or the skill set they are looking for. Usually the site focuses on complete projects of a certain complexity. Freelancers or contractors give quotations or bids for the amount that they would charge to do the job or service. Clients can select the freelancers of their choice at any time, and begin working with them.

Project4hire has freelance programmers, IT specialists, web developers, graphic artists, writers, translators, virtual assistants, HR consultants, bookkeepers, paralegals, engineers, and other freelance professionals from all over the world. Clients register onsite and post an unlimited number of projects/jobs for free. Freelancers pay a fee to accept any job or may register as a Premium Freelancer for a monthly fee and are then not required to pay the fee to accept a job. An optional Workspace is available for online collaboration and both freelancers and their clients may be rated and reviewed on site.

Full Service Platforms:

Full Service Platforms differ from the companies with Self-Service business models in several ways. As they are based in establishing long-term relationships between the clients seeking to make use of freelance talents for their remote projects, Full Service Platforms serve a strategic purpose:

- A stable of vetted and experienced freelancers are available for the company's use whenever they are required.
- The freelancer's work (and personality, reliability and work habits) are known to the Trust Broker who provides the freelancer to the company.
- The long-term relationship factor of such shared work between company and freelancer means that a body of knowledge about a company's needs and projects is built up over time, avoiding the necessity to "reinvent the wheel" with the Trust Broker

or the freelancer—everyone involved will already be on the same page from the start of any project.

- Since the trust broker both represents the company and the freelancer all knowledge acquired during the project process will be captured by the platform and be available for any future project.
- By freeing the company from the time-consuming and frustrating search for a qualified freelancer, the client is free to concentrate on other areas of their company.
- Likewise a freelancer can concentrate on his or her projects instead of locating and marketing his/herself to companies.
- The platform used assumes the role of Trust Broker, assuming the risk for the hiring and assignment of projects for both the client and freelancer.

In order for the perfect market for work to function for businesses and talent alike, only Full Service Platforms will acquire the body of knowledge needed to minimize transaction costs and to build the trust necessary to reinvent the Market for Work.

To my knowledge, there is only one Full Service Platform in operation today and we will describe it more in detail below. Before we do that, we will have a look at another concept that focuses on the business customer in a Full Service model.

Work Market

Work Market provides a software tool for large businesses to manage external work and workers, such as freelancers, contractors, and consultants in an efficient way. . As of 2013, Work Market had approximately 57,000 workers using the marketplace and 400 subscription clients.

The company markets its platform and marketplace to businesses that work with and leverage freelancers, contractors, and consultants as part of their business strategy. Most Work Market assignments are for on-site work.

Work Market allows "buyers" to find workers, verify credentials, engage and onboard talent, manage work assignments and projects, process payments, and rate workers. For workers, Work Market provides a marketplace to search and apply for assignments, share resumes, and build digital portfolios. Both companies and workers use Work Market's dashboard to manage current assignments. Workers leverage the mobile app to find and manage assignments.

People as a Service

As far as I know, <u>People as a Service</u> is the only Full Service Platform in operation at present. I am the Founder and CEO of the company.

After a more than 20-year executive career, where among other positions, I was CEO of a $160 million technology company, I became convinced that the market for work was indeed broken and could not be sustained in the future. Being in charge of the company, I imagined how I could have completely redefined our business had I had access to a global pool of trusted freelancers, to whom I could delegate part of our projects, both for strategic initiatives and for optimization. As a technology company, with ups and downs in our work assignments, I could also see how many of our best and brightest wasted many hours awaiting projects that had need of their skill set. I set out to change that.

Changes had to be made to the entire equation: how companies defined projects and found remote virtual talent to work on those projects, as well as how once full-time employees would need to become virtual freelance talent, and would therefore need an avenue to market their talents.

I knew that this global talent pool needed to be filled with workers from all over the globe and that companies would need to be reassured that such workers were vetted, recommended by a trusted company who had done business with the freelancer previously, and had the qualifications and reliability to do the job well and see it to fruition. Such freelancers and clients wishing to hire them for remote project work needed to be "introduced" and the projects explained and accepted by using the services of a middleman known to both parties. This middleman had to be someone not only known to both the client and the freelancer, but trusted by both. The concept of a Trust Broker formed and, with it, the business plan of <u>People as a Service.</u>

For their part, businesses needed to become more flexible and could no longer afford to pay idle, extraneous or unmotivated workers. They could no longer restrict their hiring to only workers within their own borders, nor require their entire workforce to report daily to the company's office site when many jobs could be done more efficiently, and less expensively, remotely.

When it came to the workers themselves, I knew that traditional job dissatisfaction was growing, with 39% of workers unhappy with their work/life balance; 45% were unsatisfied with opportunities for advancement at their current company; and that 58% of workers planning to change jobs within a year.

I was also aware that there was a market of 53 million freelance workers in the USA alone, with more people joining the non-traditional workforce every day, and that was only in one country. With the spread of technology (particularly cloud-based service) around the world, a largely untapped global workforce was available to work on projects remotely for companies, no matter where those companies were located. Such workers were often as qualified a traditional workers, but could be hired at a fraction of the cost.

Research showed me that companies who did outsource their work did so for various reasons with reducing or controlling the costs leading the list of reasons (44%). 34% did so to gain access to talent or to management resources not available to them internally. Some companies outsourced to free up their internal resources (31%), and others to accelerate a project that might be stagnating (15%).

I ventured that other companies would be willing to make use of Trust Broker concept as long as People as a Service could be shown to:

- Help the client define the job or project they needed done.
- Fully understand what the project calls for and what IS important to the client.
- Select the perfect candidate for the job.
- Make delegation of all hiring tasks easy, quick and efficient.
- Reduce the risk of wasting time on the project or in hiring the correct candidate.
- Get real and verifiable results concerning the scope, time and budget of the project.
- Follow-up on the projects on which the company, the talent and the Trust Broker have worked together.
- Build a body of knowledge about the company, their projects and the qualifications and personality of the virtual talent.
- Act as a sales and marketing department for the freelancers themselves.
- Create long-term and satisfying relationships with both sides of the equation—com-

panies and virtual talent.

- Above all—be a trustworthy and reliable Trust Broker, acting in everyone's best interests.

I knew if <u>People as a Service</u> could accomplish all those things, affordably, we would succeed. And so we have.

<u>People as a Service</u> is a new, cloud-based solution that allows companies to take advantage of the growing freelance economy. Instead of searching for traditional staffers, or looking through a large pool of untested freelancers online, companies can rely on us to connect them to the freelancer who is the perfect fit for their job. We maintain an elite stable of freelancers obtained after a global search and we keep the number of freelancers with whom we work small so that we can maintain personal and up-to-date information on each of them.

No longer are companies limited by geography (and must hire someone locally, who may or may not have exactly the skills they require), nor must they waste time and energy trying to determine if a freelancer, who looks great online, is really all they're billing themselves to be. We have worked with each freelancer we recommend on several previous projects so we know each one's talents, skills, reliability and work ethic. By keeping our freelancers working on continuous projects, we also incentivize them to "keep up the good work" in order to remain on our platform.

<u>People as a Service</u> offers a monthly subscrip-

tion for customers, with no markup on projects and no charge to freelancers. This allows the platform to be truly independent in proposing the very best freelancer for a client's particular project, as we have no stake in the money the freelancers makes. We therefore always propose the best value for customer and the customer can always trust our choice.

Our business model allows companies to delegate to us the most-time consuming and expensive and risky portions of the search for a qualified freelancer, making their choice easy and their decision upon whom to employ for a project painless. Also, as our patent pending algorithm captures and retains all knowledge gained on every project completed, companies no longer have to reinvent the wheel for each new hire. Our freelancers come equipped with knowledge of what their predecessors have done on a company's projects previously, saving time and money, and allowing the freelancer to hit the ground running.

Here are two examples of how People as a Service helped two of our clients:

A One-Woman Show

A sole proprietor had a company in the personal health sector for which she did everything: prospected for customers, designed all marketing and sales materials, handled marketing and promotion online, acted as the administrative staff, and even wrote a book on the area of his company's focus. Needless to say, she was stretched a bit thin and her efforts weren't as effective as they might have been.

The business owner had a long-running wish to refresh the social media and marketing of the company, develop a new sales program, market the new services to a new pool of potential customers and even write a new book to help attract new customers. She, of course, had no time to do any of these things, while she tried to do all the jobs herself.

She contacted <u>People as a Service</u> for help.

Over multiple months using our service, we have helped her:

- **Develop stand-alone websites for each facet of her business**, allowing each product and service to be explained in-depth the prospective customers. Each site also contains interactive features to help a prospective client see how the company's services would benefit them specifically, as well as offering testimonials, user profiles and references of clients who have used such products and services previously

- **Ghostwrite two new books**: By acting as behind-the-scenes author, editor, proofreader and marketing consultant, the books were written *for* the owner, based on telephone/ Skype interviews *with* the owner. Each book focused on a specific business-to-business problem and offered a set of solutions to those problems, helping establish the owner as a sought-after expert in her field.

- **Translate a previous book from French to English**: The owner is a native French speaker, which appealed to a European clientele, but her works needed to be translated into English in order to effectively reach an American market.

- **Proofread all web content, press releases and news articles**: The owner was not a writer and, with English as her second language, she needed the help of an experienced and English-speaking writer to work with her to craft press releases and create articles to serve as "the voice" of the company to the media and general public.

- **Complete redesign on all sales and marketing collateral materials:** Our talented freelancers acted as an in-house marketing team, where beforehand the company had none. Products were discussed, dissected and reworked for better customer satisfaction and new marketing materials envisioned and created for each product. Sales figures rose immediately.

In doing so, we have freed the business owner up to fully attend to her customers and grow her business.

An App Development Startup

The company had a great idea for an innovative app and had developed some technology but they did not have the time, staff or the financial resources develop the business. So People as a Service worked with them to:

- **Develop a leads generation project:** The client had hired several software designers to create a custom lead generation platform—an expensive and lengthy project that hadn't yielded expected results and was still unfinished months (and many dollars) down the road. One of freelancers brought her expertise to bear and presented a different and more affordable solution. By installing and making use of an off-the-shelf software product, that not only replaced the expensive custom program, but did away with the inefficient list buying solutions of the past, replacing it with an up-to-date program that culled prospects from social media and internet sources, she was able to add to and update the company's out-of-date database and generated thousands of new leads for much less money.

- **Verify the contacts in their prospect database:** Unlike the old list-based prospect rolls, the off-the-shelf solution culled leads that couldn't afford the products, were out of business, had been sold to someone else or were duplicates and discarded them. It added to the list only verified potential customers (true leads) and even assigned timed "tickle files" alerting salespeople when they should follow up with a prospect.

- **Contact those leads through telemarketing and email marketing:** Our freelancer not only installed the system, but also trained the company's sales staff in its use and how to update the software on a regular basis.

- **Provide operational support for new customers in setting up their app:** Once the company's new product was ready to roll out, our freelancers developed a clear and thorough explanation and set of FAQs to be downloaded with each app sold so new customers would be able to download and make use of the app immediately upon purchase.

- **Act as first level service for customer issues:** Anticipating some bug issues as with any new software product, our experienced freelancers were the ones who provided 24/7 service online and via live chat to new customers who experienced any problems with the app. They recorded any issues related by the customers and passed them along to the software developers in order to correct the issues, thus avoiding having to "reinvent the wheel" with each call. Simultaneously, they trained the staff of permanent employees who would act as service techs for the new product.

In both cases our customers benefited not only by meeting their goals, while freeing up more of their own time to focus on other aspects of their businesses, but created better quality work at more affordable prices. No longer squandering money on wasted efforts, both business owners found that not only more work was getting done, but higher quality work was being produced, more prospective customers were being reached, existing customers were happier and such efficiency resulted in higher profits.

Thanks to working with our global pool of talented freelancers; our patent pending machine-learning algorithm that allows us to build a knowledge bank of each of our clients' projects; our fast and flexible response to a company's needs and our affordable monthly subscription service, <u>People as a Service</u> is, in my opinion, the perfect vehicle to achieve the Perfect Market for Work.

CHAPTER 10

---

14 THINGS YOU CAN START DOING TODAY

"You may delay, but time will not"

—Benjamin Franklin, statesman, scientist and Founding Father

As a company who wants to make the best use of the new market for work:

1. Define work into smaller jobs.

Examine what it is your company does, in detail. Discover which jobs within the company truly need doing and which may be obsolete or still retained based on the premise "it's the way it has always been done". Restructure the jobs you wish to retain into smaller, result-driven activities. These smaller, more focused work content form the very basis of the future of work. No longer should there be catch-all job descriptions where a person is hired for the general ability and projects are thrown on his desk with the hopes he will have or find the resources necessary to get the job done. Work projects must be better defined and given to fully functional units to complete—whether that unit is one person or a team of dedicated people. Define the work that must be done, not the employee whose title suggests they *should* be the one to do the job.

2. Experiment with networked organizational structure.

Put aside the antiquated notion that an organization must work from the top down. The days of higher ups like remote boards of directors or dozens of managers are done. Think of your company as an organization the main purpose of which is to get things done, rather than stroke the ego (or guarantee the long career) of employees, Construct a plan about how to get the projects or tasks you've identified done in the most efficient and affordable way and think of how you might build networks around your employees, providers or freelancers that can complete those projects or tasks. Begin on a small scale. Start by selecting one team, one unit or one task (whichever makes the most sense in your organization) and strip out the hierarchical structures—the job titles and descriptions, the bosses, the time clock, the need for everyone to be onsite—whatever part of the rule book that may be hindering your attempting a different form of organization—a networked form. Then give a specific result that must be achieved. Not a goal, nor

a nebulous idea, nor more meetings to be held—
a real result, one measurable and both driven by
and in total control of the team you have assembled. Set a budget for their work and let them at
it. Observe, but don't interfere until you have to
and see how the experiment in the new future of
work model went. Based on those results, consider
expanding it to two projects or more soon.

3. Contact a trust broker and do some smaller test projects with them.

Get your first experiences with the new model
for the future of work and identify some jobs or
tasks you can give out to a freelancer through a
trust broker. First choose a non-critical job and see
how it goes. Measure the results carefully. Was the
job completed to your satisfaction? On time? On
budget? How did the freelancer work with your
existing company culture? Did the project actually
need a full-time, on-site employee? How much
time would it have cost to do the project in-house
or to hire a freelancer through a self-service platform? Compare this measurement to the trust broker approach. How easy was it to manage virtual
freelancers? Did the trust broker make it simple
to delegate finding professional and experienced
freelancers? Did the trust broker fulfill all promises made to your company? Was the trust broker
actually *trustworthy*? If your first experience with
the trust broker went well, add more tasks and

promote the concept in your organization until you think you are ready for more strategic jobs. Note carefully how smoothly ramping up the use of freelancers through a trust broker might work for even some of the largest and most important of your company's projects. Will it save you money and time? Perhaps the freelancer might actually be more skilled or have more recent experience in the field that an employee, who may not have grown in his or her job in years, but has just kept a seat warm hoping to ride the position out until retirement.

4. When a position becomes available in your company, don't do what you always have done.

Instead of turning the vacancy over to HR for them to begin the laborious process of finding, interviewing, conducting background searches, relocating, hiring and training a new employee, consider calling a trust broker and hiring a virtual freelancer instead. Consider what things a new employee would be expected to achieve if given that new position. Divide those needs into tasks that absolutely must be done by a trusted employee and those that could be given to a virtual freelancer. For the tasks that must be done internally, reconsider if any of the details of those tasks might be done by a virtual freelancer in conjunction with a trusted employee. Then outsource those tasks. See how the combination works on a small scale, one task at a time, or create a parallel process, hiring a virtual freelancer to do some of the work while your HR department is vetting the person to become the new hire. This way, you not only will have covered yourself in case the virtual freelancer experiment doesn't work fully, but will also have a stand-by freelancer with knowledge of the job waiting in the wings should your new hire or veteran employees ever need help.

5. Identify the key people you need to strategically develop your business in the future.

Consider how to sweeten the pot to better motivate them to stay. This may be in the form of better compensation, stock options, flex hours, a percentage of the business or a combination of all these things. The object is to show them how much they are appreciated and let them know that you consider them keys to the success of the business. Such core employees will become even more important in the future of work. They are the nucleus around which all the freelance atoms will revolve. Keep them apprised of your thinking. Explain to them what you have learned about the future of work and enlist them to help make that future a reality.

6. Create a financial model of your company that allows you to measure how much money your company actually spends on jobs getting done

as opposed to how much money is allocated to each department.

Start with the least complex part of your organization and use it as your model so that you can easily see the true cost of getting something done in your organization without the distraction of discretionary spending or additional budgetary line-items. You should be able to easily see that many departments are spending an inordinate amount of money without tangible results. Any jobs within those departments are probably costing the company more than is necessary. Next contact a trust broker and find out what it would cost to get those same jobs done using an outsourcing model. You are likely to see using virtual freelancers in some departments, as opposed to entrenched employees, will merit you a better result for a lower cost. Identify some of the low hanging fruit thorough your company's departments for cost savings or output improvements and start sourcing them through external sources via a trust broker.

7. Identify the strategic opportunity you always wish you had the time, financial means or strategic know-how to develop.

The future of work, with its leaner silhouette, will free up capital, open the door to a vast global talent pool of virtual workers and let you begin an in-house "start-up" based on the concept you've been considering and experiment with the results for very little investment. You will have the freedom to explore different ideas, concepts and strategies, without committing your company to bet every resource on what may prove to be the wrong horse. You will be able to experiment, try new strategies and gain knowledge and information that can be of use to your company, no matter what the outcome of the current exploratory idea. If things work out, you may find a strategic opportunity for the future and if they don't, you will have learned a lot about the model, lessons you can apply later. The future of work is the very nursery of innovation. No longer shackled by outmoded ideas or ways of working, ideas can easily grow and your company will benefit.

As a virtual freelancer who wants to become part of the future market for work, or, in fact, for anyone wanting to work:

8. Actively build your business network.

Keep in touch with friends, business associates and acquaintances in a strategic way, making the best use of technology. Handing out business cards at a networking event will no longer be enough to keep yourself and your talents on the radar of those who can help you get work. You instead need to keep up with and nourish the contacts you have and add to them in productive ways. It is the modern equivalent of staying in touch with school-mates, former colleagues and past employers—by engaging with them about how they are and what you can do for them, as well as how you are and what they can do for you. The idea of one hand washing another has never gone out of style, it as just gone into cyberspace .The use of social media as an easy way to connect, and stay connected to your network, through calls, teleconferences and emails on a regular basis is the key to your contin-ued relevancy and value.

9. Share your knowledge.

In the traditional closed hierarchy, information was power and having secret insider knowledge could be of benefit. In the future of work, the more people who know you and are aware of what you do and what you've done, the better. The larger the circle of people who think of you when they have a new job or opportunity, the more work you will get. Share your knowledge and expertise of-ten. Write a blog on your website. Guest blog for other peoples' sites. Reply to online questions. Contribute to forums in your field of expertise. Ac-cept requests from younger workers asking you to share your experience or mentor them. Say 'yes' to speaking engagements both for live conferences and webinars. Make yours a household name. Let as many people as possible see your value.

10. Build your online *and* offline reputation.

Know that everything on the internet is there forever and cannot ever be fully erased. Guard your reputation and be mindful of what appears about you online. Aim to flood the internet with positive marks about you through recommendations, evaluations, endorsements and testimonials to your good work. With such comments, your good reputation will grow. Conversely, anything that might be damaging to your reputation will also live forever in cyberspace, it is said, so you need to compensate for any one bad remark with a dozen positive ones. Begin to firmly separate your private and professional lives online. Be conscious of everything you post, as all posts have a way of becoming common knowledge. Do good turns for others online. If you find someone's work to be stellar, offer an endorsement or referral. One good turn does often deserve another. I don't recommend avoiding social media interaction to reduce the possibility of a negative comment. To do so in the new market for work is to risk invisibility and with such lack of exposure comes a lack of opportunity. Out of sight is truly out of mind in the new future marketplace. Consider instead thinking of social media as a business tool and not as a private interaction tool.

11. Throw away the time clock.

In the future market for work, no one will care if

you worked 40 hours or 4 hours, if you get good results. Some jobs will require extra effort or longer hours or weekends may become a thing of the past, but in others, your time will be your own and you'll never miss your son's softball game again. You can work at 3 am and avoid every rush hour. In the future market for work, it is much more about an all-hands-on-deck mentality. You need to be available to get the job done for the company whose project you have undertaken, while learning not to sacrifice your own personal work-life balance. Nor will the company employing you care if you achieved great results in your cubicle in the company high-rise or at home in your bedroom sitting in your pajamas. They will only care that you achieved great results. No more brownie points will be awarded just for showing up at work

12. Know thyself.

Identify what your product is—what you have to sell. What are your capabilities and experience? What particular skills or talents do you have and what have you done in your field? Factor in your education, including your continuing education. Then take the package that is you and accept projects that help you gain results and successfully complete projects based on your talents, Build your reputation and be sure to keep your successes in the public eye via social media. Find and get active in forums devoted to your vertical market. Author blog posts on the topics with which you are most familiar. Accept jobs and projects that help add to your experience. Let others see how knowledgeable you are in your field. Become an expert.

13. Realize you are a brand.

In all your social media activities, take every opportunity to sear who you are and what you do into their memories. If you are a graphic designer, become *the* graphic designer all your friends and colleagues think of when they encounter a need for someone with your skills. Make it easy for them to contact you. Keep all your information up to date online. Enlist a virtual answering machine system so you don't miss a call. Have all your email accounts forwarded to all your other email accounts. Respond quickly, even if it is only an auto-response, followed by a personal call or email. Publish articles and blogs wherever you can. Announce all business successes on Facebook, LinkedIn, Twitter and Pinterest. Write and distribute press releases about yourself. Take every opportunity to enlarge your network and engage those contacts within it. Do whatever you can to get noticed, but only in a positive way. You rarely get a change to remake a bad impression, so make a good one—and repeatedly.

14. Start now.

Time is wasting. As is evidenced by an entire generation of Baby Boomers, who thought they had safe jobs until retirement (jobs where they had worked for years and where their talents and contributions were valued and found themselves summarily let go or laid off with barely any notice), no job is guaranteed for life. Gone are the days of the gold watch and pension, so prepare yourself for the future of work. Because it is more efficient, easier to manage and delegate, but most importantly because it is more affordable, human nature (and corporate profits) dictate that every company will come around to adopting the concepts of what is called "the gig economy". You need to be on the right side of history when this happens, becoming one of those strategic employees who needs to be nurtured and kept satisfied because you play such an integral part in the success of an organization. You do not want to be the person who has been biding his or her time, riding out the clock to retirement. That clock is about to end up on the junk heap of outmoded ideas. Or maybe you do have one of the rare secure jobs but perhaps you find the whole thought of being your own boss, working your own hours and choosing your own projects an exciting prospect. Either way, now is the time to begin investigating the future market of work because the future is unstoppable and it's headed your way.

It might not feel like it today, but a Revolution is in the making, and looking back some ten years from now we will all be living in a different market for work and, with this, in a different society. We will use a different type of organization to achieve our goals and we will earn money in a different way than today.

For the first time in human history, all the elements have come together to allow for this transformation where the human potential can rise to new levels. Technology, cultural changes, new organizing principles and Trust Brokers will allow for the perfect Market for Work to form. With this will come a boost in productivity, creating of public goods and well-being for a much larger share of the world's population.

The potential this change will bring us is so enormous that it will be inevitable that it happens. We can use all your energy to resist it, however if we embrace it, we will become part of something much bigger than ourselves.

Hopefully we will all perceive this change as positive and be more fulfilled with the work (and not just cling on to a job) and work for goals where our talents will be put to best use.

CEO or simple employee, now should be the time of preparation, renewal and reimagining. Getting ahead of the curve is always better than playing catch-up. Make use of this book to lead the pack, not follow, and good luck establishing your proper place in the new market for work.

I look forward to hearing your comments and questions. Please visit: www.PeopleAsAService.co/the-future-of-work

-end-

INDEX

S

T

www.ingramcontent.com/pod-product-compliance
Lightning Source LLC
Chambersburg PA
CBHW071534200326
41519CB00021BB/6488